The K[...] Blasco Story

IT'S A Girl BUT WILL SHE LIVE?

Barbara Blasco
Marilyn Anderson

HighWay
A Division of Anomalos Publishing House
Crane

HighWay
A division of Anomalos Publishing House,
Crane 65633
Copyright 2010 by Barbara Blasco
All rights reserved. Published 2010

Printed in the United States of America
10 1
ISBN-10: 0984260501 (paperback)
ISBN-13: 978-0984260508 (paperback)

Cover illustration and design by Daniel M. Wright

A CIP catalog record for this book is available from
the Library of Congress.

For all the moms and dads
of special needs children.
May you see God's plan
for your lives.

CONTENTS

Acknowledgements   vii
Introduction   1

PART ONE
The Unexpected

Chapter One   5
Chapter Two   13
Chapter Three   17
Chapter Four   23
Chapter Five   31

PART TWO
Encouragement in Despair

Chapter Six   37
Chapter Seven   41
Chapter Eight   45
Chapter Nine   49

PART THREE
The Miracles

Chapter Ten   55
Chapter Eleven   59
Chapter Twelve   63
Chapter Thirteen   67
Chapter Fourteen   71
Chapter Fifteen   77
Chapter Sixteen   81

PART FOUR
The Plan

Chapter Seventeen   87
Chapter Eighteen   91
Chapter Nineteen   97
Chapter Twenty   105
Chapter Twenty-One   107
Chapter Twenty-Two   111
Chapter Twenty-Three   113

PART FIVE
The Lessons

Chapter Twenty-Four   119

PART SIX
No Man Is an Island

Chapter Twenty-Five   201
Chapter Twenty-Six   207
Chapter Twenty-Seven   213
Chapter Twenty-Eight   217
Chapter Twenty-Nine   221
Chapter Thirty   225

PART SEVEN
Godly Wisdom

Chapter Thirty-One   229
Chapter Thirty-Two   235
Chapter Thirty-Three   237
Chapter Thirty-Four   241
Chapter Thirty-Five   245
Chapter Thirty-Six   251

ACKNOWLEDGEMENTS

Marilyn Anderson has been a friend to our family for years. She has encountered trials and is well acquainted with those who have disabilities. Two of her brothers have special needs, and she and her husband lost twin daughters minutes after their birth. The Andersons raised five children: two boys and three girls. They consider their home to be a gift from God, and as such, it should be shared. They've opened their doors often to others. Darin Anderson, their second son, a pastor with the Evangelical Free Church, has volunteered with his family at the Joni and Friends Family Retreat in North Carolina. Marilyn enjoys going along to help care for her grandchildren. I appreciate her help in editing this book. Thanks for the many hours we've spent sharing, comparing, reordering, and rewording.

I want to thank my friend, Betty Tessien, who reviewed the book and gave me her input. Betty and her husband, Frank, have been involved in disability ministry at our church. Their son, Frank, supervised our first Wheels for the World wheelchair drive for his Eagle Scout Badge project. Betty and her family's friendship have been invaluable through the years.

Joni Eareckson Tada's organization, Joni and Friends, has been a Godsend to me throughout the years. Joni's courage in her own disability has been a source of strength to me as well as millions of others. Joni and Friends helped with the start up of H.I.M. (Hearts in Motion), our disability ministry, and they continue to be a good resource for me. I hope this book sells a million copies, as the proceeds will be donated to the organization.

There are five special women in my life to whom I will be eternally grateful. Helen Slusarz, my matchmaker, was responsible for bringing my wonderful husband into my life. She just wouldn't take "no" for an answer when she was trying to set up our blind date. Thank you for not giving up on me. I would have missed out on the best part of my life.

Another woman is Georgette Syverson. Her friendship has brought an everlasting change in my life. She introduced me to Jesus, who in return has given me the peace of God that surpasses all understanding. I am grateful to Georgette for pointing me toward my best friend for eternity.

There are three Kathryn's in my life who helped mold me into the person I am today and continue to improve the person I will be tomorrow. You will hear their stories in the pages that unfold.

Heartfelt thanks to Pastor Manny, Pastor Jay, Pastor Tony, and our church family for their support of my disability ministry. I am grateful to my friends and family who have supported, encouraged, and been available to me through all of life's trials.

Finally, I am grateful to my wonderful husband for his love and encouragement throughout our thirty-one years of marriage.

If there were one appropriate thing to be written on my tombstone, it would be:

Jesus strengthened me.
Often He used
family and friends!

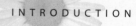

My daughter had five surgeries in the first ten years of her life. Just the fact that she survived more than the week she was given at birth was a miracle. Many wonderful things happened in those early years; even then, I felt that God was commissioning me to write a story about her life.

When Kathryn was eight years old, Richard and I received Christ into our lives. It was a simple step of obedience, but what a supernatural experience! I thought that the first eight years of Kathryn's life had been a life-changing experience for me. The years that followed, with a greater knowledge of the Bible, were even more so.

As I learned to pray for specific things, and to pray for them in the name of Jesus, I was amazed to see God working in my life. Up until then, I never had such miraculous experiences. I kept a journal of prayer requests recording how and when they were answered. My prayers were answered within minutes, hours, or a day's time. I prayed, God answered. This showed me that there really is a God, that He really cares about me, and that He would guide me every step of the way in caring for Kathryn. I wondered why God responded so quickly to all my prayers. I believe He wanted me to learn to trust Him. Up until that time, three important men in my life were big disappointments. My grandfather didn't want to have anything to do with me because I wasn't a boy and couldn't carry on the family name. My father was an alcoholic, lost in his own world of self-destruction. My first husband was a womanizer. For years, I believed in God, but felt He didn't love or care for me. After my salvation, He showed me how wrong I was.

As the years passed and Kathryn lived on, I sensed that God wanted me to write this book. Just like Moses, I felt inadequate and incapable of the task, so year after year, I put it off. When retirement came in January of 2006, I no longer had a reason or excuse to delay. It was time to follow God's command.

When Kathryn was born, I had many questions and wanted more than anything to talk to someone who had experienced what I was going through. I pray this book will answer some of the questions that mothers of handicapped children are faced with when their child is born. No man (or woman) is an island. We cannot get through the trials of disability without reaching out to someone who has been there and survived. We need to know that we can and will get through all of it. Rich and I were older and more mature than some parents of handicapped children were. That is probably why we didn't feel a great need for support groups. When we did join the Caring Parents Organization at Lutheran General Hospital right after our daughter was born, it was our intention to help other parents get through their crisis. We learned, however, that one cannot reach out to others and not glean something for themselves.

Only God has all the answers,
but if this book encourages even one person
it will have achieved its purpose.

PART ONE

The Unexpected

Consider it all joy when you encounter various trials,

knowing that the testing of your faith produces endurance.

And let endurance have its perfect result,

that you may be perfect and complete, lacking in nothing.

—JAMES 1:2-4

I felt like a fish in a glass bowl. I could see clearly out the front window, and anyone passing by could see more clearly in. After a ten-year relationship, my ex-husband Lennie dumped me in a garden apartment on a rainy day in April of 1977. He left me with a lawn chair to sleep on and a ten-year-old car with a broken transmission. I had my clothes, a pressure cooker, and a two-hundred-dollar tax refund check I had hidden from him after it arrived in the mail two weeks earlier. The empty one-bedroom apartment had no television, no telephone, and no curtains on the ground floor windows for privacy. Glancing around at my bleak state of affairs, I realized I needed to set some priorities immediately. Two hundred dollars wasn't going to go far, and it had to last until I found a job and received my first paycheck. Lennie paid the apartment rent deposit and the first month's rent, but I would eventually have to furnish it and pay my own rent.

How It All Began...

Parents, especially dads, are supposed to be invincible. When I was eighteen, my dad was diagnosed with emphysema. Doctors told him his chances of survival would be greater if he moved to a drier climate, so shortly after that diagnosis, my father, mother, and younger brother, Jimmy, left for Arizona. My older brother, Eddie, was away at college, and my sister, Pat, and I stayed in the Chicago area and moved in with our grandmother.

Life was good until three years later when my sister was diagnosed as having a "nervous breakdown." She was hallucinating and paranoid, convinced someone was spying on her. Pat was hospitalized in a mental institution for almost a year. She received thirty-two shock treatments that would forever change her life. When she got better, she was embarrassed about her illness and hospitalization. She could no longer face her friends in Chicago and chose to move to Arizona, joining our parents.

As is often the case, a change of scenery didn't alter things for my sister. Life there wasn't much better. She met her husband, Bob, and for a while things seemed to be going well. Bob had been married previously and had a five-year-old son, Peter. He was in business with his best friend for several years. My sister got pregnant with her only daughter, Suzy. Just before the baby was born, it was discovered that Bob had been embezzling money from the business. When Suzy was three months old, Bob took off and was never heard from again. With the help of my parents and the whole family, my sister struggled through raising her daughter. All the while, her mental condition was delicate.

The pressure and stress of trying to hold a job and raise her daughter caused Pat's mental illness to flair up occasionally. After being re-evaluated in Arizona, she was diagnosed with Post Traumatic Stress Syndrome, the result of witnessing an automobile accident while in the third grade. Pat was returning to school after lunch with a group of her friends. As she reached the corner, the light turned green, but she stopped to tie her shoe. Pat's other classmates continued to cross the street, and a drunk driver ran the red light, killing six of the children and just barely missing Pat. She suffered night terrors for many years after the incident. Medications, as long as she remains on them, keep her on track and allow her to lead a normal life.

While my sister was hospitalized for that year in Chicago, I started dating Lennie. He was a photographer and owned his own photography studio. He was fifteen years older than I was and a "man of the world." I was twenty-two years old and had led a sheltered life up until then. I missed my family, and I was scared to think that I would never again have the older sister I'd once depended on for guidance and direction. I transferred my dependence to Lennie and leaned heavily on him for approval, confirmation, and encouragement.

At first, dating Lennie was fun and exciting. We went to places I never dreamed of: The Playboy, Cousins', and Gaslight Clubs, and all the finest restaurants downtown. We stayed out until early morning. Sometimes he would bring me home with just enough time for me to change clothes and go to work. My grandmother didn't approve. She told me Lennie was the devil, and I should stop seeing him. By this time, I had fallen in love with him, and not dating him anymore wasn't going to happen. I moved into my own apartment. Later I would regret not listening to my wise grandmother.

Although I had my own apartment, I spent most of my time at Lennie's. I was working a full-time job and helping him with his business in the evenings. He taught me everything I needed to know about running it. The more I was able to handle his business, the less he worked with me. He started to sleep longer during the day, and he left me alone to work downstairs in the studio while he went out all night. Going out with him was almost a thing of the past. Eventually I found out that there were other women in his life. I honestly believed that if I worked hard and showed him how much I loved him, he would leave his wild life and marry me.

Then one day the IRS (Internal Revenue Service) paid Lennie a visit. They asked him why he hadn't filed his taxes for ten years. Lennie said he didn't think he owed them any money, so he didn't think he needed to file a report. He was wrong. Between what he owed them, the interest and penalties, and the tax lawyer to represent him, it cost him one hundred thousand dollars to clear up the mess. In the mid-sixties, that amount of money would have purchased three homes. We were both devastated. I got a second full-time job, working eighty hours a week, and gave him all the money I made. It wasn't near enough. The IRS put a lien on everything Lennie owned. He didn't own anything that didn't have a mortgage or loan attached to it. I worked harder to help, while Lennie turned to valium. On the drug, he slept the whole day and got up in time to go out and play at night...without me.

As Lennie depended more and more on valium, he rarely came down to work in the studio. Orders that needed final touches only he could do sat on the shelves for months. Customers were constantly calling to complain. The Better Business Bureau was frequently corresponding with us. Any incoming revenue we had was stuck on a shelf, and unpaid bills piled up. Business referrals dropped, and our number of dissatisfied customers increased. It finally got to the point that even if all the in-house orders were delivered, there still wasn't enough money to pay all the bills.

Then one day Lennie decided to apply for a $50,000 loan. For the first time in our ten-year relationship, our wedding being the second time, Lennie stepped into a church. He lit a vigil candle and prayed that he would get this loan. I thought that Lennie, in his despair, was finally turning to God, and hoped this would impact our relationship in a positive way. God answered his prayer. He got the loan. When they handed him the check, he immediately went out, bought a case of champagne and a portable television set, and took it to the bank loan officer to thank him. I thought that was extravagant as we needed every cent of that money to pay our bills. But what he did next, without my knowledge, was even more devastating. Instead of paying as many bills as possible with this money, he went out, bought a twenty-eight foot boat, and housed it at the Marina City boat dock in Chicago. I found out later he did this to impress his new girlfriend. With this purchase came even more expenses, and he doubled our debt.

During those awful days, I tried to leave Lennie three times. The last time, I sold everything from my Chicago apartment, packed up my clothes, and moved across country, ending up with my sister and niece in Arizona. I found a job at the local water company, and responsibly saved my money. When I had been with Pat and Suzy for three months, Lennie showed up in Arizona. He seemed sincere and convincing when he proposed. We got married in Arizona with my parents, my sister Pat, and my niece Suzy witnessing our wedding. I moved back to Chicago with him. Marriage to Lennie allowed me to set aside some of my guilt about living with him when we weren't married. I was also sure he would change.

When we returned to Chicago, I learned that Lennie had taken my name off of the checking account just before he came to Arizona to marry me. This gave him full control over our finances. All the years I worked for him, I wrote and signed all the checks. I had put several thousand dollars of my own money into his business, and now that we were married, he didn't trust me. I assumed he was afraid that I would take money from the account and because we were married, he would have no legal recourse to stop me.

The day we arrived home in Chicago, Lennie announced he promised a "girl friend" of his he would take her and her children to the zoo. He told me I should stay in the office at the photography studio and catch up with all the work that had fallen behind while we were both gone. I couldn't believe it!

I never knew what to expect from Lennie. One day I cleaned our apartment above the studio. I put away all the food that was on the kitchen table and picked up the papers lying all over. I thought Lennie would be delighted to see how clean and nice the apartment was when he came home. Instead, he flew into a rage, angry that I had invaded his privacy. He took the papers I put neatly away and threw them all over the coffee table and floor. "This is my apartment, not yours! Don't ever do anything like this again without asking me," he screamed.

In the months ahead, Lennie would insist I take off my wedding rings when we were out in public together. I could only wear them at home and around family and friends who already knew we were married. I always knew when he had a date with another woman because he would start an argument. He dated so many other women I lost count. I wanted to die.

Once at three o'clock in the morning, Lennie called to tell me he was on the expressway on his way home and asked if I would make him some chicken soup. I got up, pulled out the pressure cooker, and began making soup. He didn't come home that night, and I didn't hear from him. I was frantic not knowing if he was dead or alive. Later the next day, he called saying he stopped by to visit a "friend." He stayed away for three days.

When he came home, I blew up. We had a terrible argument. He went over to his desk and pulled out divorce papers. I couldn't believe what I was seeing. When did he go to an attorney to have papers drawn up? Why would he do such a thing? He started to hurl insults at me. "You're just like my first wife. You married me for my money just like she did, and you're going to take me for every penny just like she did." He spewed out the words hatefully. As he screamed, I wondered what money he was talking about. All we had were liens and mortgage attachments from the IRS. I was so hurt and angry that I signed the divorce papers he thrust at me without even reading them. Immediately he became contrite and apologetic. He surprised me by saying, "I'm sorry. Since you signed these papers so quickly, it shows me how much you care about me, and you're not after my money. I just wanted to make sure. I'm going to rip up these papers, because now I know you really love me."

In the next three months, life with Lennie was fun again. He didn't go out with other women. He took me out more. He seemed to have changed. I was happy. Then one day, I asked him if I could invite my Chicago family over for dinner. I hadn't seen them in a long time, and I missed my aunt and her family. The old, angry Lennie returned. He was livid that I would suggest such a thing. We fought. It was then that he told me we were actually divorced. He had filed the papers the day after I signed them. I didn't have a lawyer, I never went to court, and I wasn't told anything. I found out later the reason why he kept our divorce a secret. Legally I had thirty days after the papers were filed to contest the divorce. Lennie didn't want me to know we were officially divorcing so I wouldn't get a lawyer and enter a contest. It was also part of his scheme to be nice to me the last three months, so I wouldn't suspect his motives.

Lennie's scheme was successful, and I was numb, but, ironically, I wasn't furious. In those ten years together, any love I'd had for Lennie had evaporated. I was empty of love, concern, and feelings. The past few years, I'd felt as if I was in prison and had received a life sentence with Lennie. Now he was offering me more than parole. I was getting a pardon! I grabbed it. I told him I wanted to get my own apartment. If I wasn't good enough for him to be married to me, I certainly didn't want to live with him. I was thirty-two years old, and I could start over. I was free at last, and life would be good again.

CHAPTER TWO

Though I was relieved and felt free, I also felt alone and terrified about my future. How was I going to go to my family after they had told me over and over again that Lennie was a mistake? I was going to have to make it on my own. The mess belonged to me, and I needed to get myself out of it. I was mad. Mad at myself. Mad that after all I had done for Lennie, this was how he repaid me. It was this anger that drove me the next year of my life. I determined I would show Lennie I didn't need him or any other man in my life. I'd pick myself up and get my life in order, if for no other reason than to prove to him and to myself that it could be done.

After Lennie dumped me in the fishbowl, I shopped at K-Mart for the basics. I'd taken so much for granted all my life! Anything I needed was always just there. I'd never really paid attention to how vital even the little necessities were. I purchased a shower curtain, a washcloth and towel, a bar of soap, shampoo, toothpaste and toothbrush, and a hairbrush. I bought shades for the windows; they were cheaper than curtains. For the kitchen, I bought dish soap, a small sponge, canned soups and food, some paper plates and bowls, and one plastic cup. When my bill was paid, fifty dollars remained. That would be gasoline money for job hunting. My pressure cooker would have to work for heating up my food.

As I was returning home from the store, my car stalled in an intersection. Cars were beeping at me as if I purposely made the old thing stop right in the middle of the street. I finally got the clunker moving again. I knew the transmission had to be fixed soon; it was dangerous to drive the car the way it was. I got to a pay phone and called my friend who was an auto mechanic. Dennis had fixed Lennie's cars for years. I didn't know how I would pay him, but I needed an estimate to see what it would cost to fix. Dennis came over to look at it. The verdict was that "Clunker" was bad and needed to be fixed immediately if it was to remain at all functional on the road. He said he would repair the transmission, and I could make payments. Many years and fixes later, Dennis and his wife, Georgette, have become lifelong friends.

God was watching over me as I got the first job I applied for at Dynascan Corporation. The pay wasn't the best, but it was enough to pay my rent, my household bills, buy me some food, and take care of "Clunker" expenses. However, if I was ever going to have furniture besides a lawn chair, I needed a second job. After a month working at Dynascan, I applied at Sears and got an evening job in the Customer Service Department. It was a couple of blocks from home, and the hours were perfect. I stashed away this extra cash for three months and paid Dennis in installments for the transmission. Then I began to save money to buy a table and chairs for my dining room. A couple months later, I had chairs and a place to eat my meals sitting down.

July 19th was my cousin Debbie's birthday party. It seemed the perfect time to begin to rebuild the relationship with my family. I had ten dollars and some change to my name, and one week until payday. There was food in the fridge, and my bills were all paid, so I bought a birthday card and put the ten dollars in it. I wasn't so much afraid of not having any money left as I was of how my family would respond to me when I showed up at the party. This would be my icebreaker.

When I arrived at their house, my reception was warm. I felt like the prodigal daughter returning home. I broke down and sobbed. I finally admitted to my family I was divorced, and I had been living in an apartment nearby for several months. I didn't tell them I was sleeping on a lawn chair and had no telephone; they found that out for themselves.

My uncle and his brother owned a gas station just two blocks from my apartment. Uncle Chester stopped at my apartment one day to invite me over for dinner, as I still didn't have a telephone. He was shocked to find that I had very little furniture. My aunt's friend, Dolores, came over with a wooden table and chairs for the kitchen, items she found in an alley. My uncle brought over an extra sofa chair from their house. Another friend brought over a mattress and springs. There was no bed frame, but it was a lot more comfortable than the lawn chair. She also brought a bed-room dresser. I never felt more loved in my entire life. Life was starting to pick up for me; it was going to be good! With each new addition, the apartment was starting to look more like home.

One year later, I had replaced all the used furniture with brand new things, had a telephone and television, and even bought a new car. I felt proud of myself. My self-esteem improved, and life was getting better every day.

CHAPTER THREE

One day a friend, Helen, invited me over to her house for a swim. She lived two blocks from my apartment, so I walked over. It was the beginning of my new life but I didn't know that yet. Helen was trying to fix me up with a blind date. It was with a guy named Rich who worked with her at the Chicago Sun Times Newspaper. She kept telling me what a nice guy he was. I kept telling her, "I'm not interested." After a few months and much nagging, I agreed to go on one date with this "Mister Wonderful."

Richard took me to a Polish restaurant on that first date. We had a good time, but he was quiet and didn't seem to have much of a sense of humor. He was nice, but I didn't think I could be happy with someone who wasn't more outgoing. As far as I was concerned, though, it was just a date, nothing more.

I was happy when Rich brought me home and didn't try to kiss me. He was a gentlemen; I had to give him that.

I knew I would have to account to Kay, a new friend I'd met at Dynascan. We had so much in common that we became fast friends in a relatively short time after I started working for the company. Kay became my best friend, and a friendship ensued that lasted over twenty-seven years. Kay would want a full "Rich" date report the next day.

A week later, Kay invited me to dinner and ordered me to bring Rich. I told her I didn't think that was a good idea. I hardly knew the guy, and I didn't want him to think I was getting serious with him, which I wasn't. Kay, however, always won an argument. We had a gourmet dinner. The saying about "the fastest way to a man's heart is through the stomach" must be true. By the look on his face and the way he ate, Rich was in seventh heaven.

The phone was ringing as I walked in the front door after that wonderful dinner at Kay's. Rich dropped me off, and Kay was calling before I stepped foot in the door.

"Honey, he's a very kind man. You'd better marry him. You could probably marry someone richer, or more handsome, but you will probably not find a kinder man. Grab him." Kay spoke so emphatically that I dissolved into giggles.

"Should I wait until he proposes first?" I asked when I finally caught my breath.

Kay told me she could see in his eyes he was in love with me, and it would just be a matter of time until he declared his undying devotion! Kay was hopelessly romantic!

No matter how I tried to deny the obvious kindness of this man, my friend's words stayed with me. With her advice in mind, I accepted further dates from Rich and watched him carefully. He bought two season tickets to the theater for us. He was very caring, but I still didn't think that his personality was what I needed and longed for. After five months of dating, Rich proposed to me one evening. I told him I cared for him, but I reminded him of how deeply I had been hurt and said that I needed time to think about it. The look on his face showed the rejection he was feeling. I tossed and turned the whole night. Rich was the kindest man I had ever met. He obviously cared about me, and I knew in my heart I cared about him, too. Of course, I was afraid to make another mistake. I was determined not to be a two-time loser.

Kay's words kept coming back to me. It was as if God Himself was telling me that whole night, "It's okay, Barbara; it's in My Plan for your life. Don't be afraid."

The next morning, I called Rich at work first thing at nine o'clock. He answered the phone.

"I accept."

"Who is this?" he blurted out.

I laughed and said, "So, how many women did you propose to last night?"

We both laughed. He asked what made me change my mind.

My answer was a surprise to Rich. "I said I needed time to think about it. I thought about it, and I'm accepting your marriage proposal."

Contrary to what I thought on our first date, in the six months of our engagement I learned Rich did have a great sense of humor. He just needed to feel more comfortable with me. We had tickets to go to the theater on the night I accepted his proposal. We stopped at a Burger King for a quick sandwich before the show. Rich was quieter than usual.

I decided to bite the bullet and asked, "Is something wrong? Are you having second thoughts about marrying me?"

"No, it's just scary, that's all."

"Marrying me is scary? Thanks a lot."

"I didn't mean it that way. It's more like your first car accident. You don't know what to expect."

"How complimentary! You're comparing our marriage to your first car accident?"

That totally broke us up. We looked at each other and laughed until our sides ached.

A couple weeks later, Rich and I went to a movie. About an hour into the movie, Rich's work beeper went off. Beepers back then were rare, and, of course, there were no cell phones, so he got up and went to the lobby to call work. While he was gone, a girl sitting behind me said to her friend, "He must be a doctor." I giggled, and when Rich returned I whispered what the girls said. Without hesitating and in a loud whisper he said, "He dies, he dies, I'm not missing the end of this movie." I've always thought that those girls were thankful he wasn't their doctor.

Helen, the friend who introduced us, couldn't understand why I thought Rich didn't have a sense of humor. He was funny at work, and the two of them had been in social situations. The day of our wedding, Rich painted the word "HELP" on the soles of his shoes. As he knelt down by the altar, people in the front pews giggled. I didn't know why until later that day.

On our early dates, he didn't want to say the wrong thing, but soon the real Richard was exposed. There was not a doubt in my mind as I walked down the aisle on April 9, 1978.

Kindness is one of Rich's strong points. Every day during our honeymoon, my new husband would ask, "What would you like to do today? This is your honeymoon." Every day I would laugh at his jokes. What he said to me that last day in Hawaii would be published in the June 1989 "Reader's Digest." Holding my hand at a romantic restaurant on our last night in Hawaii, he said, "Honey, this has been the best two weeks of my life. I just want you to know that if you ever leave me, I'm going with you!" Even though it sounded funny, and I laughed, the look in his eyes showed how serious he was. I often teased afterwards that it made no sense to ever leave Rich; he would just follow me.

Rich and I were home from our honeymoon, and I decided for both of us that we needed to lose weight. I made a diet-friendly meal, and after eating our healthy dinner, we went to the 5 & 10 Cent store. I needed to buy some yarn. When we got to the store, Rich said he'd like to wait for me in the car. I told him I would be a while, but he still insisted on waiting outside. In the store, I went from aisle to aisle looking for the yarn. It was not in the usual area. I asked a clerk where the yarn section was. She told me that they discontinued yarn. I left the store disappointed.

Arriving back at the car earlier than expected, Rich had a startled look on his face. He sputtered, "I thought you said you would be a while?"

I answered, "They discontinued yarn, and we have to go to another store." A puzzling look of relief crossed his face. I learned what it was about as I sat in the passenger's seat and felt warmth on my heels coming from somewhere under my car seat. I reached down and pulled out a brown bag containing two hot dogs. Suspiciously, I glared at my new hubby and asked, "What is this?"

He replied, "I was hungry, so I bought *us* a hot dog."

"What are they doing under the seat, and when were you going to tell me about them?" I responded. We both laughed, but even that early in our marriage, I knew Rich couldn't be totally trusted when it came to food.

CHAPTER FOUR

I got pregnant shortly after our two-week honeymoon in Hawaii. Our families were overjoyed. We could hardly wait to hold our baby. My bridesmaid, Abbie, asked how I got pregnant so fast, as she had to wait fifteen years to have her first and only child. Rich jokingly told her, "Cheez Whiz." She never did figure out how Cheez Whiz helped, and Rich never made it clear to her that he was just kidding. I've often wondered what she imagined.

We chose baby names. It was to be Brian if he was a boy and Kathryn if we had a girl. Kathryn would be named after my grandmother and my new best friend, Kay. I liked the name Kathryn; it meant "strong." Both my grandmother and Kay were very strong women. They were both survivors.

Even huge snow mounds left by the worst snowstorm in years didn't stop Kathryn's baby shower from taking place. The shower was given by my bridesmaid Abbie and my friend Pat. Parking was almost impossible with so much snow still covering so much of the street. People ended up parking on a main street that had been cleared a block down from the house.

Richard joked so much about naming a baby boy "Arco," after my Uncle Chester's gas station, that the cake said, "Welcome Little Arco." This child would have a great starter wardrobe. One of my friends, "Auntie Terry," bought ten outfits. She was only one out of the thirty people who attended the shower.

Our baby was due on my birthday, March 5. As the due date came and went, we patiently awaited her arrival. Finally, the doctor told me that he wanted to take protein samples from my urine. For three consecutive days, I had to drop off urine samples at the doctor's office. On the evening of April 2, I got a call. My doctor wanted me to come to the hospital. It was time to induce labor. Protein levels in my urine were too high. The doctor thought there was a problem, but he never let me know about his concerns.

Immediately after arriving at the hospital, I was rushed to the x-ray department. The doctor called Rich out of the room. I was too pumped up about delivering the baby and too naïve about birthing and possible complications to realize that there could even be a problem. It had been ten months of pregnancy and I wanted it to end. Rich came back into the room with an odd expression on his face.

"What's the matter?" I asked him.

"Nothing," he insisted.

"Rich, be honest with me. I can see something is wrong. It's written all over your face. I can handle it."

"The baby's head is small."

"Aren't all babies' heads small?"

They had already induced labor and the pains had started. Richard was relieved that I didn't push him further. I had my work cut out for me just to deliver our baby. Later, I learned that the doctors showed Rich the x-ray which looked like the baby's head was in two pieces. They didn't expect the baby to live after birth, and had been frank with Rich about this possibility. In the delivery room, they put me under for a few minutes until the baby was out. Kathryn was born five minutes after midnight on April 3, 1979. When I woke up, I saw a blurry figure and a bright light shining on me.

"It's a girl…but she won't live," said a voice.

At first, I wondered who the voice was addressing. Certainly, no one was talking to me! The words didn't sink in until a few minutes later. Eventually, as the anesthesia wore off, I could see it was my obstetrician talking to me.

In the recovery room, I asked to see my baby.

"I don't think it's a good idea. Neither does the doctor," Rich replied.

"Neither you nor the doctor had this baby. I did, and I want to see her."

What seemed like an hour or so went by when they finally brought in this little baby wrapped in a blanket with a knitted bonnet on her head. Though she was a month late and was twenty-one inches long, she only weighed five pounds.

At the time, I saw none of that. I said, "She looks beautiful. What's wrong with her?"

How does one break such news to a new mother? Rich spoke as gently as he could. "It's under her hat. It's her head." I could see tears spilling out of Rich's eyes.

"Remove the hat, I want to see it," I said.

Rationally, Rich tried to reason with me saying, "I don't think that's a good idea." I argued that it was my child; I needed to see what was wrong. I told him that I couldn't go my whole life not knowing why my child died. The hospital staff shook their heads no. Their refusals only made me angry. I demanded that I see her head. When they took that little knitted bonnet off, a bonnet probably made previously by some hospital volunteer, I couldn't believe what I saw. There was her little head with this "tumor" sticking out in the middle. I knew then that they were right; she couldn't possibly live like that. The occipital encephalocele, though I didn't know that terminology at the time, had part of her brain in it, and the whole mess was infected. She had severe microcephaly, again a term I was unfamiliar with then. The doctors felt that the infection would spread throughout her body and that she would die within a week's time. They said that even if she did live, she would be a vegetable in a fetal position the rest of her life. There wasn't much hope.

That night was so long. I wanted to scream and cry out loud for my little girl.

I didn't dare. I had a roommate, and I mustn't keep the new mom next to me awake. She needed her rest to take care of her healthy newborn baby. I was relieved to learn she was leaving the next day. Then I could cry and be myself. The hospital staff was very sensitive and they didn't give me another roommate through the duration of my stay.

Dr. Henry Mangurten was in charge of the NICU (Newborn Intensive Care Unit). He was gentle, tactful, and kind; the perfect man to deal with the highly emotional situations that dominated this unit. He chose his words carefully, trying not to add more stress to an overwhelming experience. I knew him enough to feel I could trust him with Kathryn's life.

Later that day after Kathryn's birth, they brought her into my room for her bottle-feeding. The nurse came in after an hour to get Kathryn and take her back to the NICU.

"Could I hold her just a little longer?" I asked, fighting back tears.

The nurse smiled and nodded kindly. She agreed saying, "Sure, I'll come back later for her."

The television was on, but my eyes were fixed on my tiny

angel who wasn't going to be with us for long. I held her and prayed that God would give me more time with her. She looked so peaceful in my arms. A couple of times, she opened her blue eyes and made me smile. I questioned why God was going to let my baby die. I rationalized that it must be my fault because of my sinful relationship with Lennie.

A few hours later, the nurse returned to get Kathryn. "I really need to get her back to the NICU now." It was ten o'clock. I had held her for nearly four hours. She had been perfect the whole time. Not a peep out of our newborn daughter.

I reluctantly gave my small bundle up to the nurse.

After the nurse left, the news came on. One of the news items of the day was about a woman who tried to drown her newborn child in a toilet in one of the restrooms at the Woodfield Shopping Center in Schaumburg...just a few miles from the hospital. She would have succeeded if another woman had not come into the restroom and seen what she was doing. The mother put the baby boy down on the floor and ran out. I don't know what the rest of the story was because at that point I was screaming at God. How could God give a perfectly healthy baby to someone who didn't want him, and give me a child I desperately wanted but who wasn't going to live? God made no sense to me at this point, and I very angrily told Him so.

Later I pleaded with Rich to tell me why God would do this.

"God wants Kathryn more than we do," he answered.

I got mad again, this time at Rich!

Frustrated, I said to my husband, "God doesn't want Kathryn more than we do. He just has more to say about it than we do."

Each day of her stay at the hospital, I asked the nurses if they had her birth certificate ready. Somehow, I felt that that piece of paper was going to be the only thing I would have left of Kathryn after she died. I was obsessed with getting it. I nagged and nagged the nurses until it was finally brought to me. I look back now and think of how silly I behaved, but at that time, it was the most important thing in the world to me...*proof that I had a baby.*

Being so wrapped up in my daughter's situation, my recovery after her birth was definitely secondary. I don't remember pain or discomfort for my own healing; I was numb. I checked out of my own room and stayed with Kathryn in the NICU twenty-four hours a day. I held her as much as the staff would allow. She was so fragile and tiny. Every time I looked at the blue lettering on her white t-shirt that said, "Not to be taken out of the hospital," it made me sadder. I knew the words meant the t-shirt, but I could only recall the words of the doctors that Kathryn would never leave the hospital. I realized that she would never get to wear all the beautiful clothes she had received at her baby shower such a short time before.

On day two of Kathryn's life, I asked Dr. Mangurten if I could bring her own clothes and put them on her. He looked at me, puzzled.

"No one ever asked me that before," he said looking confused. He hesitated, not knowing how to respond. "Sure, why not," he finally answered. "But whatever you bring will have to be sterilized first before they are brought into the NICU."

Not knowing how one would sterilize baby clothes, I asked, "How should I sterilize them?"

"Just bring them here and we'll do it," he reassured me.

I went home immediately, picked out five new outfits, and brought them to the hospital. Each day after that, I put a new outfit on Kathryn's tiny body. Soon I saw other parents bringing in their own clothes for their children in the unit. I had started a new trend in the NICU.

On Sunday, six days after Kathryn was born, Rich's mother and his sister, Marilynn, were coming to visit. I had only one clean outfit left for her. It was a yellow outfit with dark blue embroidered lettering near the left shoulder that said, "Take me home." I cried as I dressed her ,thinking that going home was not an option for this lovely little child I had grown to love so dearly in such a short time.

Rich brought the camera and we took a lot of pictures of Kathryn after we dressed her. To our surprise, the head nurse came over. She asked, "What are your plans for Kathryn?"

I heard what she said, but I didn't know what she meant. What future plans could we have for a daughter who, according to the medical team, was not going to live long? The nurse went on. "Kathryn is doing really well, and Dr. Mangurten doesn't see any reason to keep her in the NICU or in the hospital any longer. Have you made arrangements with a facility, or are you planning to take her home with you?"

I was in total shock. I couldn't believe what I was hearing. Of course, I wanted to take my baby home with me, but I wasn't prepared for that responsibility after only six days. How would I take care of her head? I wasn't a nurse. Mixed emotions raged through my mind. I was told a nurse would teach me how to care for her head, and I could call the NICU, day or night, if I had questions or any problems. We started gathering her things together to go home. The nurse not only showed us how to clean and care for her head, she gave us bandages and cleansing meds to take with us.

We called Rich's mother and told her not to come since we

were bringing Kathryn home. As I reached down to pick up Kathryn and put the blanket on her, Rich smiled. "We should have put this little 'Take me home' outfit on her six days ago. It worked."

We both laughed and were overjoyed as we carried Kathryn out to the car that Sunday afternoon. Against all the odds, our baby was going home!

CHAPTER FIVE

Dr. Mangurten called first thing on Monday morning to ask how we were doing and how Kathryn was. He told me if we needed anything at all, day or night, to call the NICU. He also mentioned there was a support grief group and asked if we would be interested in attending. When I told him we were interested, he said he would have the pastor in charge call me.

A couple hours later, Pastor Sharon called and invited us to the support group that met once a month. They were meeting the following evening at the hospital. I told her Rich and I would be there. I hung up, but immediately called back asking if the other parents brought their children and if we could bring Kathryn with us. There was an uncomfortable silence.

Pastor Sharon finally said, "That's an interesting question. All the other parents have lost their children, but maybe it would be good for them to see Kathryn."

It was my turn to feel awkward and uncomfortable. I wasn't sure that I wanted to bring Kathryn under those circumstances, but Sharon insisted. It turned out to be a wise decision.

We attended our first group meeting the next day and for nine months after that. Every parent came each month just to see how Kathryn was doing. They wanted to hear what was going on with her. Each month we would share our story and, believe it or not, these parents felt they were better off than we were. They had lost their children, but their children were at peace. They didn't have to go through all the ordeals that Kathryn was going through. For them there were no weekly visits to the doctor and runs from one hospital to another for various tests and treatments. These parents were glad they didn't have to nurse fevers and worry that any day without warning it might all be over.

The grief group was a real education for Rich and me. One of the mothers told how, in her denial, she bought clothes and fixed up the nursery after she gave birth to a stillborn baby. She said no one wanted to talk about the baby she lost. Her family and co-workers avoided the subject. Her husband was grieving too, but didn't want to talk to her about the baby. The worst part for her was that after the baby was born, she never got to see or hold her child. She didn't give her child a name, and her husband had the hospital dispose of the baby's remains. In her mind, this baby had never existed. It was a couple of months later that she and her husband named the baby and held a memorial service. With that simple service, she was able to accept her loss and turn from her grief.

By November of 1979, Kathryn's encephalocele was growing alarmingly larger. The pressure on her head was causing her discomfort, and she was fretful and wakeful day and night for close to a month. I called Dr. Mangurten. He suggested I bring her into the hospital so the nurses and doctors could observe her, and we could get a good night's sleep. Dr. Raj, a neurosurgeon, came to examine her. His recommendation was to remove the encephalocele, though, according to him, she had a 40 percent chance of surviving the operation. We decided that this would have to be done sooner or later, so we agreed to the surgery.

The infection on Kathryn's head was so severe that the surgeon wanted to wait until it was completely gone. Medicine and treatments helped, but signs of infection remained. After waiting two weeks, Rich and I asked Dr. Raj to do the surgery as soon as possible. Kathryn had the encephalocele removed and her head closed on December 18, 1979, nine months after her birth. We brought her home from the hospital on Christmas Eve, definitely our best Christmas present ever.

Each woman in our support group got pregnant again and delivered before Kathryn's surgery. The group gathered for the last time in January to see Kathryn after her surgery, and then our support team broke up. Ironically, each mother had a child of the same sex as her child that had died.

The grief group opened my eyes to the importance of going through the grieving process. I realized how important it is for both parents to talk about the child they lost. It promotes healing. I learned the importance of naming a child no matter how long he or she lived. I learned the five steps of grieving and how important it is to go through them without getting stuck in one of the stages too long. From childhood, our parents protect us. We sometimes grow up thinking there is a bubble protecting us from harm. Eventually that bubble bursts, and life slaps us in the face. If the resulting disappointment is a death or a disabled child, the tight security of our world is challenged. The grief group helped me accept that life would never be the same. I needed to go through the grieving process completely. Thankfully, I learned this. Helping others to find comfort through their grief would become a goal for me.

Our monthly meetings for those nine months were invaluable. It opened doors for me to be able to share what God taught me through adversity. I can empathize with other parents of disabled children, something that only those who have been in the same situation and felt the same fear, anger, and hurt can do.

PART TWO

Encouragement in Despair

And he set the priests in their office and encouraged

them in the service of the house of the Lord.

—2 CHRONICLES 35:2

CHAPTER SIX

Through the years, Richard and I have experienced many words and gestures of encouragement from family and friends. These began immediately after Kathryn's birth. As friends and relatives heard of our situation, their responses overwhelmed us. Such support continues to give us the strength to care for all her needs.

After Kathryn's birth, while I remained in the hospital with our baby, Richard took the responsibility of calling our family and friends to give them the news of our baby girl. Upon hearing his voice, their first response was, "That's great! Congratulations!" Rich then had to tell them that our daughter wasn't going to live. When he came back to the hospital, he told me he had only called a few of the people on our list. Making the phone calls was the hardest thing he ever had to do. He felt like he was building up hopes with the statement that we had a girl, and then as quickly as he got them excited, he heard the let down when he said she wasn't going to live. I suggested that he tell everyone the way we were told, "It's a girl, but she won't live." At the time the doctors said this, we didn't give it much thought as we had bigger issues to deal with.

When I told people those were the first words we heard from the doctor after Kathryn was born, our friends said it was an insensitive way for the doctor to give us such distressing news. In hindsight, I know there is no easy way to tell a parent their child isn't going to live. The doctor's blunt statement was quick and painful, but a slower, long, drawn out explanation would have been just as hard to accept.

The first week I was home from the hospital with Kathryn, I got a lot of calls and visits. Our friends and family were in shock, as we were. My aunt told me that a close friend of ours, Dorothy, wanted to call, but she didn't know what to say. If we were going to keep our close friends, we were going to have to make them feel comfortable, so I called Dorothy and told her that it was a hard situation, but we would get through it. I told her I understood how hard it was for her to call us, and I probably would have felt the same if the tables were turned. She was glad I called. A couple of weeks later, Dorothy held our daughter when she smiled for the first time. Even Kathryn knew we needed to encourage our friends.

On Tuesday of that first week, my friend Abbie visited. She didn't bring her daughter Heather with her. I asked her why.

With tears in her eyes she said, "How can I bring my healthy daughter here when your daughter isn't going to live?" With her usual honest concern, she added, "How will you feel about Heather after your child dies?"

Knowing my friend needed consolation, I paused before sympathetically saying, "Abbie, I can't spend the rest of my life avoiding children just because my daughter died. I'm not going to cross the street when I see a mother walking toward me with her healthy child, or turn off the television when they show a baby commercial. My life will go on no matter what happens. What kind of a friend would I be if I felt bad that you have a normal healthy child? I'm happy for you and I'm glad that you have Heather. I will be upset with you if you keep her away from Rich and me."

Rich and I quickly saw that our reactions and encouragement to our family and friends was as important as their support to us. Abbie's response pointed out that our friends shared our concern and grief.

CHAPTER SEVEN

My friend Mary Jane visited us also, and she brought us a pound cake. Her simple, caring gesture was a great encouragement to us. In taking the time and effort to make and bring that cake, she showed us support and concern. Caring gestures leave no doubt of a friend's kindness and consideration; those gestures also demonstrate to the grieving ones the empathy that friends feel. Mary Jane was obviously distressed that our daughter was going to die, and we appreciated her concern.

Mary Jane and I played cards together in our ladies' group. We girls got together occasionally to play cards at each other's homes. Two weeks after Mary Jane's visit, we were scheduled to meet at her house. She suggested we wait until "something" happened before we continued getting together. I knew she meant well, but Kathryn was already two months old and doing well. It reminded me of something my mother said to me several years before when doctors believed my dad wasn't going to live through the night. I asked Mom if she was planning to bury my dad in Chicago or in Arizona where they lived at the time.

"We don't bury the living! Your dad is still alive. If and when he dies we will talk about where we will bury him, and not until then!" Mom said sternly.

41

Dad lived almost sixteen years longer. So, when Mary Jane suggested we wait until Kathryn died before meeting again, I politely told her I wasn't putting my life on hold until my daughter's death. I suggested we play cards as planned. Our daughter is still alive thirty years later. I thank God for reminding me of the wisdom my mother expressed. It helped me get on with my life.

During those first few weeks and months of Kathryn's life, God graciously showed me the importance of family and good friends, and how trivial material things were. He also showed me how much He cared about me.

Before Kathryn's birth, I was cynical about all the bad things happening in my life and in the world. People seemed detached; they didn't really seem to care about each other anymore. Doctors like television's Marcus Welby certainly no longer existed. It appeared to me that the medical professionals were more interested in their Mercedes and attaining a vacation home and a boat to go with it than they were about their patients' health. People didn't seem to have time for each other. The world was getting more and more materialistic. I included myself in my disillusionment.

Many of our friends were married years before Rich and me. We saw how hard-working and accomplished they were with their nice homes, cars, wonderful vacations, and more money than we figured could possibly be necessary. I idolized their lives and lifestyles. As the world counted, I had nothing most of my life. Now, however, I was married to Richard and soon we would have all the same nice material things as our friends. My plan for after my child was born was to put him or her into day care and go back to work. It would be no time at all before we were caught up with our friends. After all, I rationalized, look at all that I had accomplished in just one year after my divorce. With two salaries, Rich and I could do a lot more a lot quicker.

In short order, however, the birth of our disabled daughter changed my thinking. Money, cars, *things* didn't seem important when one is faced with the death of their firstborn child. Not only did my attitude toward our finances change, I also began to look at doctors and people in a different light. The doctors at Lutheran General Hospital, Dr. Henry Mangurten, Dr. Raj, Dr. Nadu, and others who came to see Kathryn that first year of her life, were the most kind, loving, caring doctors I had ever met, and I am forever grateful.

People we never met sent gifts to Kathryn. My aunt Bernice worked at a drug store in Chicago. Richard, Kathryn, and I visited Aunt Bernice, and she handed me a stuffed animal. She had shared with one of the customers in the store about Kathryn, and the woman came back the next day with this gift.

Another time, my sister bought Kathryn a birthday gift. At a store in downtown Scottsdale, she found a soft, fuzzy animal for her. While shopping, she struck up a conversation with a clerk in the store. She was the owner of the small shop. Pat told her that her niece, Kathryn, wasn't expected to live much longer. A package came in the mail, and I called my sister to thank her for the gifts. I scolded her for buying so much; it was too expensive for my sister's budget. Our conversation confused Pat. She had only bought one small thing for Kathryn. The owner of the store filled the box with other gifts, a thoughtful gesture toward Rich, Kathryn, and me.

These two strangers enriched the lives of Kathryn, Richard, and me. Their sympathy impacted me so deeply that I wanted to spread the thoughtfulness. When Kathryn was alive and well at one year old, I became active with the "Caring Parents Organization" at Lutheran General Hospital. I volunteered to be a support parent to other parents of disabled children. Dr. Mangurten would call me to inform me of a grieving parent. He asked me to call them. After making an appointment, I would pick up a stuffed animal to comfort them as we had been comforted. It was a small gesture, but it was always appreciated.

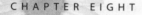

CHAPTER EIGHT

God has a back door way of teaching us. Newspaper, radio, and television point out a small example of the way people treat others in this world. The news media often focuses on stories of violent, bad things. There is an entirely different side of life that isn't usually shared. Having seen only the media side had made a cynic of me. God showed me the compassionate, caring people in the world through Kathryn's birth and life. There are many more wonderful people in this world. Because of Kathryn's disability, my faith in mankind has been restored.

Loving, caring encouragements were continually bestowed on our small family of three. These were in the form of gifts, cards, telephone calls, visits, a home cooked meal, newspaper articles, and poems. One friend came over with a serenity prayer plaque. I had not seen this prayer previously.

SERENITY PRAYER

GOD, grant me the serenity to
accept the things I cannot change,
courage to change the things I can,
but dear GOD, please give me the wisdom
to know the difference!

That plaque hung over the changing table in Kathryn's bedroom for years and now hangs over her bed. It's still a reminder that only God can change us. He may not change our circumstances, but He will change our attitude if we allow Him to take control.

Another encouraging poem arrived in the mail on a particularly low day. The down days were not so few and far between at first. As time went on, the low times became less frequent. God seemed to know when I needed cheering up, and it helped when friends and family recognized these low points in our journey with Kathryn. Once my Aunt Bernice was visiting her daughter in the hospital and read the following poem from a bulletin board. She copied it down and mailed it to me. For many years, people told me I had a special child. I thought it was their way of being sensitive to our situation. It was not until I opened this letter and read the poem that it was impressed upon me that caring for Kathryn was part of my mission in life. I felt I was getting a glimpse into my future as the caregiver of our special child as I read the words, with a warm feeling in my heart.

HEAVEN'S VERY SPECIAL CHILD

by Edna Massimilla
© 1956 Hatboro, Pa. 19040
reprinted with permission

A meeting was held quite far from earth,
It's time again for another birth.
Said the angels to the Lord above,
This special child will need much love.

Her progress may seem very slow,
Accomplishments she may not show.
And she'll require extra care,
From folks she meets way down there.

She may not run, or laugh or play,
Her thoughts may seem quite far away.
In many ways she won't adapt,
And she'll be known as handicapped.

So let's be careful where she's sent,
We want her life to be content.
Please Lord, find the parents who,
Will do a special job for you!

They will not realize right away,
The leading role they're asked to play.
But with this child sent from above,
Comes stronger faith and richer love.

And soon they'll know the privilege given,
In caring for this gift from heaven.
Their precious charge so meek and mild,
Heaven's very "Special Child."

I always loved and valued my aunt and uncle, but never as much as after Kathryn was born. Uncle Chester worked at his brother's gas station just a few blocks down the street from where we lived. Often he would stop by to see me. One day he said, "Call Richard and tell him to come to our house for dinner tonight, then pack up Kathryn and your dirty laundry and I'll pick you both up in twenty minutes." Just his words and hearing his voice gave me a lift.

We had a laundry room in our apartment building, but I didn't want to leave Kathryn alone to do our laundry. One thoughtful gesture by my aunt and uncle was allowing us to do our wash at their house.

CHAPTER NINE

Good advice was not always encouraging to me during Kathryn's early years. My life-long friend, Charlotte, and my mother-in-law, Rose, both had their own thoughts about Kathryn. Though their help was well intentioned, I didn't understand or appreciate what they implied.

Charlotte had a son, Richard, who was born with Downs Syndrome. Richard was in his twenties. My husband and Richard would do trivia questions for hours on end trying to outdo each other. Richard was working part-time for the Park District in their hometown. He was high functioning, polite, considerate, and loving. I told Charlotte that I would be happy if Kathryn was able to do half as much as Richard.

Her response to my comment shocked me. "Oh no, Barb, you don't want that for Kathryn. Although Richard is smart, well mannered, and holds a part-time job, he knows he is different from his sister and brothers and other people. He has been hurt many times by unkind people. But Kathryn will never be hurt by unkind words or stares. She will be safe in her own little world where she will only know love and kindness."

My mother-in-law said something similar to me. "In many ways, Kathryn is a lucky girl. She doesn't have to worry about

grades in school or who she is going to marry. She doesn't have
to worry about getting a job, or cooking, cleaning, and grocery
shopping. She's being cared for. She will never have all the responsibilities in life that we have to deal with. She is to be envied. She
has two great parents who love her and take good care of her."

My friend Charlotte encouraged me that Kathryn will never
be hurt by anyone. My mother-in-law pointed out that Kathryn
has a good life just the way she is. I didn't see these words of
wisdom as words of encouragement when they were first spoken,
but as the years have gone by, I see they were both right. I watch
mothers of other handicapped children and even healthy children. They have many more problems to deal with than we do.

In Erma Bombeck's book, *Motherhood: The Second Oldest
Profession,* she dedicates a whole chapter to "The Special Mother."
A few years later, she used this chapter in her newspaper article
and renamed it "The Valiant Mother." In March of 1982, when
Kathryn was three years old, my sister sent me this excerpt from
her book.

This year, nearly 100,000 women will become mothers of
handicapped children. Did you ever wonder how mothers of handicapped children are chosen?

I visualize God hovering over Earth selecting His
instruments for propagation with great care. He instructs
His angels to make notes in a giant ledger.

"Armstrong, Beth, son. Patron saint, Matthew.

"Forrest, Marjorie, daughter, Patron saint, Cecilia.

"Rutledge, Carrie, twins, Patron saint...give her
Gerard. He's used to profanity."

He passes a name to an angel and smiles, "Give her a
handicapped child."

The angel is curious. "Why this one, God? She's so happy."

"Exactly," smiles God. "Could I give a handicapped child a mother who does not know laughter? That would be cruel."

"But has she patience?" asked the angel.

"I don't want her to have too much patience, or she will drown in a sea of self-pity and despair. Once the shock and resentment wear off, she'll handle it.

I watched her today. She has that feeling of self and independence that are so rare and so necessary in a mother. The child I'm going to give her has his own world. She has to make it live in her world and that's not going to be easy."

"But, Lord, she doesn't believe in you."

"No matter. I can fix that. This one is perfect. She has just enough selfishness."

The angel gasps, "Is selfishness a virtue?"

God nods. "If she can't separate herself from the child occasionally, she'll never survive. Yes, here is a woman whom I will bless with a child less than perfect. She doesn't realize it yet, but she is to be envied.

"She will never take for granted a spoken word. She will never consider a step ordinary. When her child says 'Momma' for the first time, she will be witness to a miracle and know it. When she describes a tree or a sunset to her blind child, she will see it as few people ever see my creations.

"I will permit her to see clearly the things I see— ignorance, cruelty, prejudice—and allow her to rise above them. She will never be alone. I will be at her side every

minute of every day of her life because she is doing my
work as surely as she is here by my side."

"And what about her patron saint?" asks the angel.

God smiles. "A mirror will suffice."

After reading this, I called my sister and thanked her for sending this to me. I told her it made me feel good and lifted my
spirits. I loved it so much that I framed it and hung it next to
the "Serenity Prayer" plaque in my daughter's bedroom. It wasn't
until later, though, that I realized that other parents of disabled
children weren't as happy with this article as I was.

PART THREE

The Miracles

Trust in the Lord with all your heart,

and do not lean on your own understanding.

In all your ways acknowledge Him,

and He will make your paths straight.

PROVERBS 3:5–6

CHAPTER TEN

As Christians reflect about past events, we sometimes wrongly view God's miracles as merely good luck. When we know God is in control of everything in our lives, though, even in the small details, we see how He arranges mighty miracles for His children, not simply good luck. With open eyes and hearts, we can truly experience and appreciate His good works.

Miracles were, and still are, abundant in Kathryn's story. After talking with Dr. Mangurten, Rich and I decided early on we would not allow the medical team to perform extraordinary means to keep her alive. Since the doctors agreed she was going to die anyway, we didn't want to prolong any suffering. Dr. Mangurten backed us in this decision. At six months old, she developed a high fever and started bleeding rectally. She had a red, blotchy rash all over her body. We were scared and didn't know what to do. My aunt called, and insisted we call the doctor or take Kathryn to the emergency room. Feeling very guilty after that phone call, I called Dr. Mangurten and told him the situation. His advice was to keep Kathryn home through the night, and if her fever and bleeding persisted to bring her in the next day. Kathryn's fever broke during the night, and the bleeding completely stopped.

Early the next morning, Dr. Mangurten called asking how Kathryn was doing. He said, "I suggested you keep Kathryn home through the night, knowing if she wasn't strong enough, all the machines in the world wouldn't keep her alive. If you'd brought Kathryn into the hospital, they would have attached her to all kinds of machines. People would have said the machines helped her survive." Through this and other medical situations, God taught us another lesson during Kathryn's first illness; God, not machines or medical technology, determines life or death.

Doctor Mangurten warned us that if the encephalocele on Kathryn's head ever completely collapsed she would probably die from the shock it would cause to her body. When she was seven months old, the unthinkable happened. The encephalocele broke while I was feeding her one night. Crying, I woke up Richard and told him to call the NICU and let them know what happened. A few minutes later, Dr. Mangurten called back. Knowing that the hospital would resuscitate her, he was kindly frank. He advised us to keep her home until she died and then bring her in to the hospital to have her declared dead. I held Kathryn that whole night praying for a miracle. God answered. The pockets of fluid on the encephalocele began filling up. By morning, it was back to its original size. When I talked to Dr. Mangurten the next morning, he couldn't believe what a survivor our little Kathryn was.

In her first ten years, Kathryn survived five surgeries. She had pneumonia twice the first two years. She was hospitalized eight times for her surgeries, pneumonia, and therapy. Her hospital and doctor bills were over a million dollars, but God provided through our insurance companies.

I took a leave of absence a month before Kathryn was due rather than quitting my job at Dynascan. Had I quit, my insurance coverage would only have been good for thirty days. Since

Kathryn was born a month late, neither of us would have had adequate coverage. One of the owners of Dynascan approved continued insurance for the entire year I was off work.

When I returned to work on a part-time basis, my supervisor, Bill, informed me that as a part-time employee, I wouldn't be entitled to insurance benefits. I laughed. "You mean the company covered me the whole year I was off, but now that I'm back, they'll terminate my plan?" He was surprised to hear this, and they didn't take away my benefits, another provision from God.

Years later, I learned that my friend, Kay, intervened and insisted that the owner, her direct boss, keep me on the company's insurance plan.

CHAPTER ELEVEN

When Richard and I were certain Kathryn was stable, we moved from the city to the suburbs to get Kathryn in the "0-3 Program" for disabled children. It was an exciting step. Kathryn was progressing, and in our new neighborhood, she would get into a program that would help her physically, socially, and emotionally. I called Judy, the head of the program, whom I'd met several months earlier at one of our support group meetings at the hospital. "We've moved to Niles, and we're ready to put Kathryn into your program," I said.

Judy sounded distressed as she said, "I'm sorry, Mrs. Blasco, but we have a waiting list of seventy-five children ahead of Kathryn. We won't be able to take her at this time."

When I got off the phone, I called Rich at work and cried. However, the next day Judy called back. "Mrs. Blasco, I checked the entire waiting list, and of all the children on the list, Kathryn would benefit the most from our program at this time. Please bring her in tomorrow and we'll get her started."

When Kathryn turned three, she began to attend Julia Molloy, a private school for special needs children. She needed a wheelchair so that she could be picked up by the school bus every day. The wheelchair was designed to make it easier to travel with a handicapped child. The back wheels of the chair could be removed so we could lift the whole chair onto the front seat of our automobile. Kathryn used this wheelchair until she turned twelve and needed a larger, more conventional chair.

The new chair, however, would not fit into our car. We needed a van, but we didn't have enough money to purchase one. I asked Richard if we could cash in some of his company stock for a down payment on the van.

Rich checked with his boss about the stock price and requirements for cashing them in. His boss told him not to make that transaction until the next week. There were rumors the stock was going to split. We waited and, sure enough, the stock split. Rich went back to his boss, thanked him, and asked his advice again. His boss repeated his advice of the week before for the same reason. It split twice in two weeks! By waiting, we were able to double the down payment for our van.

That's not the end of the story. Our neighbor had contact with a local Chrysler car dealer, so he helped us get the best price. After we bought the van, I asked the dealer if he knew where we could get a wheelchair hookup for the new van. He asked why we needed one. When we told him our daughter was disabled, he told us about a $500 rebate through the Chrysler Company. He referred us to a shop that did specialty work installing disability equipment.

The next day, I called the place he recommended and asked what they would charge to install a wheelchair hookup in our van. $499.00. Does God play "The Price Is Right?"

Was it *good luck* or *God?* If you really believe in God, the word luck shouldn't be in your vocabulary. Though I was grateful and amazed for all the help and support, I wouldn't see God's hand in any of these situations until years later when I asked Jesus into my heart. It was then that I realized He was the source of all that help and support.

CHAPTER TWELVE

As Kathryn grew, we took her out of the crib and bought a twin bed. However, the twin bed was not practical or appropriate for a special needs child. Aching backs were the result of bending low to change her diapers and clothes. Even though the bed had side rails, she often fell through the rails and part way onto the floor. It was dangerous, but we didn't know how to fix the problem.

At five years old, Kathryn had to be hospitalized for surgery to realign her hips. While in the hospital, I was confident she was in a safe bed, and it was easy for us to change and maneuver her frail body, a help for aching backs. On the day she was going to be released from the hospital, I was awake early to pray. Rich and I had just pledged a substantial amount of money to our mission's ministry at church. As I prayed that morning, I had a question. "Lord, maybe we shouldn't have pledged so much money to missions. Instead we could have used it for a new, safe hospital bed for Kathryn." As soon as the thought was uttered, I bit my tongue and told the Lord I was sorry for being selfish. I had to trust that when Kathryn needed a new bed, God would provide it for her. I should have known that God would take care of all our needs, and His methods would be amazing.

Around noon, the hospital social worker came into our room and asked if there was anything she could do for us before we went home, or if there was anything we needed at home. I responded jokingly. "Yes, I would like to take this hospital bed home for Kathryn."

After I explained our set-up at home, the social worker nodded. She said, "The insurance company would probably give you a hospital bed for several months until Kathryn's cast is off and her therapy is over."

"I would like to have the bed permanently," I pressed, though I knew that something was better than nothing.

The social worker shook her head. "They'll never approve that."

I nodded and agreeably said, "I'll take it for as long as the insurance company will allow."

By three o'clock in the afternoon, I had not heard anything from the social worker, and the doctor hadn't signed release papers. At the front desk, I asked the nurse when the doctor was going to release Kathryn.

She answered, "The doctor had an emergency this morning and he just arrived. He will be signing her release papers in a few minutes, Mrs. Blasco."

Hearing my name, the woman next to her inquired, "Are you the Mrs. Blasco that requested a hospital bed?"

After I assured her I was, she said, "The insurance company approved a hospital bed for Kathryn for six months." She probably figured she was giving me good news, but I was disappointed.

Giving myself a pep talk, I thought, "Six months is better than nothing, Blasco!" For some reason, though, I continued to push. "I really need the bed permanently. My back hurts from changing her, and the bed we have at home is unsafe. Besides, the doctor said that she would probably need another operation in six months."

Though she was doubtful, she agreed to try to convince the insurance company to approve our request. She said she would get back to me.

A mere fifteen minutes later she came into the room and with a smile informed me the bed was ours for as long as we needed it. Kathryn still sleeps comfortably in this wonderful gift from God.

Rich and I were new Christians and we began to see how God cares about every aspect of our lives. When we do God's will with our finances, God provides everything we need. Connecting with a good Bible-teaching church helped us see life through God's eyes.

CHAPTER THIRTEEN

As Kathryn continued to grow, she needed a third wheelchair to suit her needs. We didn't anticipate a problem with the insurance company. They paid for the first two wheelchairs. However, the insurance director focused on each detail and the mechanics of the chair. He was willing to approve some of the cost, but not the entire amount. He said that some of the items we ordered were not necessary. Looking over his list, we wondered which parts of Kathryn's chair would be "not necessary." He listed straps for her waist, shoulders, and feet as unnecessary items. He felt that arm and thigh pads were not necessary. According to the director, even brakes for the wheelchair were deemed unnecessary.

I tried to contact him several times to ask why he wouldn't authorize payment on these things as they were all approved on her previous chair. He wouldn't give me a straight answer, and eventually he stopped taking my calls. I wrote letters, but he didn't respond to them either.

The following Wednesday, I attended prayer meeting at our church and asked for prayer that this director would change his mind and approve the whole wheelchair. The cost was around three thousand dollars, and we didn't have that money in our account.

The following Sunday, the head elder in our church gave me a check for three thousand dollars saying the Board agreed to pay for the wheelchair from the Elder Fund. In tears, I thanked him. This generous donation was appreciated, but I refused the kind offer. I replied, "I'm deeply touched that the elders would consider paying for the chair, especially since we just recently started attending the church, but I can't take the check. It's the responsibility of the insurance company. They paid the whole cost in the past, and they should pay the whole cost now."

We were adamant that we weren't asking for anything more than what Kathryn had previously. The director was being inflexible, but I felt he would eventually decide in Kathryn's favor.

The elder said, "If you change your mind, let me know. The money will still be available for you if the insurance company won't pay."

This was confirmation from God that, one way or the other, this wheelchair would be paid for, and I shouldn't worry.

Ironically, or maybe not so ironically, the insurance director's assistant, Pat, was a born-again Christian. She had been Kathryn's nurse in the NICU when she was born. She told me that she couldn't understand why her boss was being so hard-nosed about this. She said she was praying he would reverse his decision.

She prayed. We prayed. Our friends at church prayed. And God listened. Two months went by, and still, there was no wheelchair for Kathryn. Then one day Pat called. "Your wheelchair payment has been approved," she said. She sounded as excited about this as I was.

When I recovered from shock I asked, "What made the insurance director change his mind?"

"He didn't. They fired him. The first piece of paper I put

under the new director's nose was your wheelchair request, and he approved it immediately," she laughed.

I laughed also. "If that director knew he was up against the Lord and not just the Blascos, he would have signed that paper without hesitation."

I couldn't wait to tell Rich and the church Elder Board the good news.

CHAPTER FOURTEEN

Our small, two-bedroom house in Niles was no longer suitable for Kathryn's third and largest wheelchair. The rooms were so small that the wheels would hit the furniture as we wheeled her from the front door to her bedroom. The wheelchair was too large to get through the kitchen door. Kathryn had to eat all her meals in the dining room. It was also harder for us to carry Kathryn into the bathroom to bathe her. We looked into different kinds of lifts for her, but none were right for our house.

Then, unexpectedly, in 1996, my niece called me from Arizona saying she wanted to move to Chicago. She asked if she could stay with us until she got settled in her own place. Richard and I thought this was an opportunity to get to know her better. Up until then, we'd only spent a week or two at a time with Suzy. We only had a two-bedroom house, so a bigger house made sense. We decided to look for a three-bedroom house so Suzy could have her own room.

Rich lost his job at General Binding Corporation due to cutbacks. He was out of work for a year. Fortunately, he collected severance pay for nine months, and the entire year he did some consulting. He finally landed a full-time job with the local telephone company, however his yearly salary was sixteen thousand dollars less.

We were concerned we wouldn't be able to manage our household with the substantial cut in pay, but we were surprised when he got his first paycheck. It was only a little over a hundred dollars short of his former take-home check from General Binding.

Richard looked at me as if I was crazy when I suggested we start looking for a larger home to accommodate Kathryn's needs. He sputtered, "I'm getting sixteen thousand dollars a year less, and you're saying we should look for a bigger house?"

"I feel the Lord is directing us to a new house. Would it hurt to just look around?" I reasoned. I smiled sweetly and he agreed.

The Sunday after we made the decision to do a house search, we asked for prayer in our Sunday school class that God would open or close doors to show us His will.

The following Thursday I got a call from Patty, one of our Sunday school class members. She asked if we would like to come and look at her house as they were thinking of moving. Her parents were moving out of state, and Patty and Tom wanted to buy their larger house in the same suburb.

I was hesitant, not wanting to disappoint my friend. "Patty, we're looking for a ranch house with open rooms to easily move Kathryn's wheelchair around. We have something very specific in mind."

"Come and look at our house to see if it's a fit." She was persuasive.

We did. It was a ranch with open rooms, which was one of our requirements. There was no garage and the family room was downstairs which would have made it difficult to enjoy that part of the house with Kathryn, a definite negative feature. It was bigger and so was the lot, definite pluses. Patty and Tom encouraged us to look around before we decided. They gave us their asking price and we all sat down at their kitchen table and prayed. We asked God to show us His will.

During the week, we looked at a lot of homes. None of them fit our needs. Assessing each, we could see Patty's and Tom's home would fit our needs best. We would be able to buy the new house for only $9,000 more than what we would ask for our house. Interest rates were down, so we checked into mortgage rates. We found that by making this move, our payments would be almost five hundred dollars less than what we were paying on our current mortgage. This seemed to be an open door from the Lord.

We prayed that our house would sell quickly, and we'd get the exact amount we needed to make the move. We went to a friend's house for dinner the following Saturday and told them of our intentions to move. Arlene mentioned that her sister's in-laws were looking for a house in Niles. We called them. They came over, asked how much we were asking, and gave us a check for the down payment. We couldn't believe how God just kept opening the doors for our move, but we shouldn't have been surprised. After all, we did pray for God to open or close doors!

God intervened more after we moved into our new home. Rich came home a couple weeks later and told me about his promotion. His new salary was higher than what he was making when he left GBC.

Patty and Tom moved into her mother's five-bedroom house, and a month later she found out she was pregnant with their fourth child. It appeared that God knew far better than they did that an extra bedroom was going to come in handy.

My niece lived with us for a year and a half. In our previous home, we would have been too crowded to accommodate Suzy and all her things. In the year and a half, it was a blessing when Suzy received Christ into her heart.

Sharing one's home can be gratifying. Suzy wasn't the first "Blasco boarder." Having a disabled daughter didn't deter us from opening our hearts and home to others. Though Kathryn was only nine years old, we volunteered to host two Christian Russian refugee families. One family of three, a couple and their eight-year-old son, came and remained with us for a year. They left and the wife's mother, father, and an adult sister came for six months. All of our Russian friends came with only a couple of suitcases, so they didn't need a lot of room, and our hide-a-beds in the downstairs family room in our old, two-bedroom home, were sufficient. Larissa and her parents cared for Kathryn and cooked meals for Richard during a time when I needed to be in Arizona attending my father's funeral. This was their way of showing appreciation and it was a blessing for us.

Shortly after we moved into our new home, Rich learned he was fully funded in the savings plan from the General Binding Corporation. We received a check for his portion from GBC a couple of months after we moved in. This money had been taxed so it was ours, free and clear. We were able to put an addition onto our new house almost immediately. The old kitchen became a dining room, and a kitchen/family room combination was added. That provided us with a second family room on the ground floor. Kathryn could be with us upstairs all the time. An attached garage and enclosed porch made the house perfect for our needs.

Walter, our contractor for the addition, was an unexpected bonus. Not only was he kind and generous, but he and his wife, Lucina, also had a disabled child; another Kathryn. We two couples formed an immediate connection because of our mutual experiences with our handicapped daughters.

Walter's daughter, Kathryn, was more severely retarded than our daughter was. He loved our Kathryn and could relate to our situation and the challenges of being a parent of a special needs child. With him as our contractor, not only did he bond with us, we didn't need to explain as much. He understood.

Walter's first bid on the addition was more than we anticipated, but he said he would work with us. He wanted to do this job for us. After starting the work, he did more than was called for in the contract. Instead of putting a roof just on the addition, he did the whole house. This was unexpected and appreciated as the roof on the house needed to be replaced. One day after our addition was finished, he put in an electrical outlet in our garage at no charge.

If Kathryn was not off to school by the time Walter's workers arrived for the day, he wouldn't let them use the saw because the loud sound it made frightened her. He would tell them to find something else to do until the bus came. Today we are still good friends. His friendship is another one of God's miracles for the Blascos.

CHAPTER FIFTEEN

While Walter's men worked on our new addition, I decided to go on a week-long mission trip with Joni Eareckson Tada's organization, Joni and Friends. Our "Wheels for the World" team delivered wheelchairs to people in Poland. I wanted to go, and Rich encouraged me. An added bonus allowed me to remain in Poland an extra week to meet with my European relatives for the first time.

About a week before I was supposed to go on the trip, Kathryn started acting strangely. I was suspicious she might have a urinary tract infection, so I took her to the doctor. They took a urine test and were shocked to see the sugar level in her urine was way too high. If it was determined that Kathryn was diabetic, she needed to be in the hospital, but first a blood glucose test was necessary. We went home and waited for a call with the results of the test.

Just thinking about Kathryn being diabetic was distressing. Diabetes would be a difficult challenge! Controlling diabetes would be another complication we didn't need to deal with on top of Kathryn's other handicaps. Kathryn only ate what she liked, and only when she was hungry. Regulating meals on a strict schedule, as diabetics must, would be tricky, and maybe impossible. The situation was nerve wracking, especially since I was due to leave for Poland in a week! I called our church and asked them to put out a telephone prayer chain that Kathryn didn't have diabetes.

The doctor called a couple hours later and said that Kathryn was not diabetic, but the high quantities of sugar in her urine could be a sign of a kidney problem. He gave us the name of a kidney specialist and told us to make an appointment with him as soon as possible.

The next day, when I called for an appointment, the receptionist said that the earliest we could come in would be in three weeks. My maternal pushy nature kicked in, and I told the receptionist my daughter was severely retarded, and she seemed to be in pain. After consulting with the doctor, she told us to bring her right over. The doctor fit her into his schedule that day.

Rich and I took Kathryn to the office, and the first thing they did was take another urine test. We waited while they got the results. We heard the doctor talking to the nurse outside the examining room door. He was saying, "I don't know how to tell them this. I guess I should just tell it the way it is." Our hearts skipped a beat as the door opened.

The doctor looked confused as he gave us the result. "I don't know how to tell you this because it doesn't make any sense. Your daughter's urine shows no sign of sugar in it. Looking at yesterday's test results, it is impossible that her urine is normal today. It takes a couple of days for that amount of sugar to leave the system; it's not possible for it to be normal this quickly. It's like a miracle."

I smiled. "Of course, it's a miracle, doctor. Our whole church prayed that our daughter wasn't diabetic."

He shook his head. "I can't argue that. I don't have any other explanation for it."

A week later, I left for Poland with Joni and Friends, at ease knowing that Kathryn was okay. We never had another problem like that again.

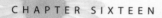

CHAPTER SIXTEEN

Kathryn's big day finally arrived! It was another of those God-sent miracles in her life. Our little girl was graduating from Julia Molloy. For me, it was a twenty-one year dream. I promised myself if the Lord allowed Kathryn to live to graduation day, we would have the biggest party for her. After all, this would be the only big event in her life. She wouldn't graduate from college. There would be no bridal shower, no wedding, and no grandkids. This was the biggest event in her life and we were going to do it up right.

We would rent a big white tent and have it set up in our back yard. The day would be beautiful and sunny, not too hot, not too cold. Kathryn would have a beautiful graduation dress. I would cook the special meal myself. Our whole family and lots of friends would be invited, including the whole church. It would be perfect. It would be the grandest party. I knew God had brought her this far, so nothing was going to go wrong on that special day.

A month before graduation day, we got a notice from the Village of Morton Grove announcing the street would be torn up to put in new and larger sewers. Being optimistic, I hoped they would be completely done with our end of the street before the party. Not so!

The week of the party, the construction crews dug deep trenches in the street next to the curb. We couldn't get in or out of our driveway. We were hoping the holes along the curbs would be filled by the end of the week so our guests could park on the street. However, two days before the party I went grocery shopping and had to drive over the parkway lawn two houses down to get to our driveway to unload the van of the food I had bought.

The day before the party, the arrival of the tent presented a major challenge. The deliveryman insisted the tent was too heavy to carry from the corner to our house. The workmen were accommodating and made a temporary bridge for him to get his truck into our driveway. I asked the foreman of the construction crew if they would have this trench filled in by the end of the week in time for my party. He said that would be impossible. I felt panicky. Close to two hundred people were coming, and there weren't going to be any parking places! Then, after enduring so much for the past twenty-one years, I dissolved into tears.

Being resourceful, I called the Mayor of Morton Grove to see if he could help me. I explained I'd waited twenty-one years to see my daughter graduate, and how the doctor said she wasn't going to live a week when she was born. I told him how I had planned this day for years, and now that it was here, my whole street was torn up and Kathryn's party was going to be ruined.

The mayor graciously listened and did not interrupt the hysterical woman on the phone line. Finally, when I was done speaking, he gently replied. "I understand completely. I had two disabled children who died. I realize how important this day is to you. I'll call the supervisor of the job and tell him to fill in the trenches for this weekend. I hope that you have nice weather, and that your party will be a big success."

Almost speechless, I found my voice and thanked him profusely.

When the street crew left on Friday afternoon, the trenches were filled in. The workmen left behind one grateful woman.

To top it all off, my niece was getting her master's degree the same weekend as Kathryn's graduation party. She asked Rich and me if we could come to two ceremonies. On Friday night, she was going to get a special commendation. Saturday morning was her graduation ceremony in downtown Chicago at Navy Pier. She assured us that the commencement exercises would be over by noon; and I would be home early enough to cook all the food for Kathryn's party on Sunday. At that point, I wished I'd hired a caterer to handle the whole affair, but the food was purchased. I was committed. There was nothing I could do except proceed with our plans.

The graduation ceremony ran longer than expected. We waited until Suzy got her degree, and then we left. Our day was not over. It was almost three o'clock, and her friend was having a party for her. It would be rude not to attend.

Traffic out of Navy Pier was terrible. We didn't move for almost an hour. It was nearly four o'clock, and I still hadn't arrived home to cook. Thankfully, my friend Cate and some other friends offered to help and were already cooking up a storm at our house. After checking the progress at home, I went to Suzy's party for a short visit. I stayed up most of the night preparing food for the next day.

That night the weatherman predicted rain.

"It won't rain on my daughter's parade!" I staunchly announced to Rich. "God held back the rain for our wedding day. He will do the same for Kathryn's important day!"

Sunday morning it rained cats and dogs. Gusty winds took down part of the tent. The grass was muddy. The rain messed up some of the tables, and all the chairs were wet. Rich was sympathetic.

I was confident and insisted, "Don't worry Rich; God will clear the weather in time for the party."

When we got back from church, the weather was already better, and as usual, God came through for us. By two o'clock, the sun was out, and everything had dried up. The food was cooked and delicious, and the tent was repaired. The tables looked great with colorful tablecloths and fresh flowers. The party went off perfectly as scheduled. Kathryn looked beautiful in her new party dress. It was a beautiful party by anyone's standards, and our guests enjoyed every minute, staying well into the evening.

We only got a couple of pictures of this wonderful party, but it didn't matter. Nothing could ever spoil or take away the good memories of that long-awaited day.

God has placed so many loving, caring people in our lives. Friends, our mechanic, social workers, waitresses, a church elder, a Sunday school classmate, a house contractor, construction crew workers, even the mayor of our town have all been used by a great and loving God to make our time with Kathryn enjoyable and a witness to the world. It doesn't matter what someone does for a living, if they make themselves available, or even if they don't, God can and does use everyone to fulfill His purpose!

PART FOUR

The Plan

For I know the plans I have for you
declares the Lord, plans for welfare and not for
calamity to give you a future and a hope.

JEREMIAH 29:11

When Kathryn came home from the hospital and was a couple weeks old, I prayed and asked God to let her live until Mother's Day. It was less than a month away, so I didn't think this was an unreasonable request. Selfishly, I wanted at least one Mother's Day with our little girl. When that prayer was answered to my satisfaction, I prayed again and asked God to let her live until Father's Day. Again, it was just a month away and Richard was such a good father that he deserved to have one Father's Day with his baby daughter. Father's Day came and went, and I thought that maybe God would grant one more wish, Christmas. What is Christmas without a child? Surely, he would grant me one Christmas with our only child. That milestone arrived. I'd received positive answers to all three prayers. I decided it couldn't hurt to ask God for "just one birthday." Obviously, God also granted the birthday prayer request. Thirty times as of 2009! Kathryn has had thirty birthdays. Praise Him!

The Bible says if we ask anything of God that is in His will for our lives, it is already ours. I didn't pray Kathryn into living this long; God already had it in His great plan for her life. God doesn't make mistakes. He has a plan for each and every one of us. We each have our own unique destiny. God will reveal His great plan for your life day by day, moment by moment. Ask Him to show you your individual life-plan.

At first, I didn't know what God's plan was for my life and for Kathryn. However, as I prayed and trusted, He slowly unveiled His plan to me.

God's unveiling started right after Kathryn was born, but we didn't realize it then. We were involved in a grief group during the first year of her life. The hospital where she was born had a second support group called "Caring Parents Organization" (CPO). Rich and I started going to meetings once Kathryn had her head surgery and was stable. The group met once a month at the hospital, and we were involved for about three years.

Dr. Mangurten asked if I would be willing to be a referral mom for mothers who had children in the NICU at the hospital. I was pleased he asked. He told me there was a baby in the NICU who had been born with a stomach deformity. She had no skin over her belly, and no one expected her to live. Her stomach was exposed and was badly infected. I agreed to help.

Dr. Mangurten gave Frankie our phone number, and a few hours later she called. I agreed to meet her at the hospital cafeteria that evening. When Rich got home from work, I ran to the store and bought a small, stuffed bear and headed for the hospital. Frankie was twenty-five years old. We talked for an hour over a cup of coffee. Frankie hugged that tiny bear the whole time. When we finished chatting, Frankie said; "Thank you! You just said everything I've been feeling, but haven't been able to express." We became friends in an hour.

That day, after our talk, I visited Frankie's baby in the NICU nursery. She was in an incubator. Her stomach was uncovered; the infected area was black. Frankie said, "You don't have to look. I know it's not very pretty." I assured her that Jessie was beautiful, and after looking at Kathryn's exposed head for almost one year, seeing her daughter didn't bother me at all. It was true, and I meant it.

A month later, I received a call from Frankie. She was crying. "They want to take Jessie off the respirator. The doctors say she isn't going to live. I don't know what to do. What should I do, Barb?"

Thankfully, the right words came to me. "Frankie, there was a girl named Karen Quinlan. She was on a life-sustaining machine for a long time and her mother wanted to take her off. The hospital wouldn't allow it. The mother took the case to court and won. They took Karen off the machine. To everyone's great surprise, Karen lived ten years after that. What I'm trying to tell you, Frankie, is that God, not any machine, is keeping Jessie alive. When God feels that it's time to take her home, no machine in the world will help."

Frankie and her husband allowed the doctor to disconnect the respirator. She rocked Jessie in her arms until she died less than an hour later. She was sad. She had peace about their decision, but it took some time for Frankie to accept Jessie's death.

Later, I learned that Frankie was related to my uncle's nephew by marriage. I also found out that she got pregnant and had a beautiful, healthy boy two years after Jessie died. After losing her first-born child, it took her time to decide to try again. Today, she is a mother of three healthy boys.

I didn't know it then, but this relationship with Frankie and Jessie was God's way of giving me a glimpse into our future disability ministry.

CHAPTER EIGHTEEN

In 1994, a man in our church, Robin Norris, approached me one Sunday morning with a question. "Would you consider starting a ministry for the disabled in our church?"

His request caught me off guard; I hadn't thought about such a ministry. It didn't take me long, however, to weigh the idea. I said, "That would be something that I would like to do, but, to be honest with you, I wouldn't know where to begin."

Robin was ready for my hesitant response. He suggested, "Pray about it and ask God for wisdom and direction."

From that short conversation with Robin and then after a few longer ones with God, our "H.I.M." (Hearts In Motion) ministry was born. It was slow starting, but each time I got discouraged, God sent me encouragement. I met a woman with a Downs Syndrome daughter at Moody Bible Church's Founder's Week. She invited me to speak at their support group at Wheaton College Church. I was excited, but nervous about giving my testimony to almost a hundred people. Robin's wife, Naomi, went with me and sang a song called, "Where There is Faith." That song made me realize that, without faith, we have nothing, but with faith, nothing is impossible. Not only the song, but also the whole evening confirmed my decision to start up a ministry for the disabled at our church.

Speaking at the Wheaton church gave me courage and confidence that I could speak to groups of people, but starting a ministry seemed different. I prayed, asking God if this was His will for me. He needed to make that clear to me, and I needed guidance.

The day I uttered that prayer, the Lord made my decision clear. I received a letter from Steve Jensen, an associate of Joni Eareckson Tada. Joni and Friends was considering opening a Chicago branch. Part of their purpose would be to educate and support churches as they established disability ministries in their community.

I attended a meeting with about thirty other people, and Steve presented the purpose and plan for Joni and Friends chapters. While he was still speaking I thought, *Sounds good, Lord, but I don't know any disabled people in our area. How am I going to get disabled people involved in this ministry?* No sooner had I had this thought than in the middle of his presentation, Steve suddenly stopped and pulled out a piece of paper. He said, "Before I forget, I got a call from Cee Cee. She has a disabled daughter and is looking for a support group in her area. Does anyone here live in the neighborhood of Dempster and Harlem in Niles?"

I nearly fell off my chair. The intersection of Dempster and Harlem was six blocks from my home. I needed confirmation, and God certainly gave me a full quota. I surrendered my will to God's. If He chose the middle of Steve's presentation to immediately answer my concern, a ministry to the disabled is where I would aim. After several meetings with Steve Jensen, our pastor, and elders, our church was the first to start a ministry for the disabled under the guidance of the new Joni and Friends Chicago office.

I visited Cee Cee and her twenty-one year old daughter

Gina, who had significant special needs. A support group would be appropriate to help Cee Cee deal with issues that came with her daughter's recent disability, but an effective support group required more participants. I knew that this was a beginning for the new ministry I had in mind.

The people fell into my lap! While running errands, I pulled into a parking spot, still wondering how I could get more disabled people involved. As I got out of my car, a woman asked where I got the lift for my van. She had a disabled son and was looking for a van with a lift. We talked, and I told her I was considering starting a support group. She gave me her telephone number and hurried off. There was my second contact!

The same day, after I left the grocery store, I had a letter to mail. I went to the post office, mailed the letter, and drove to the side of the parking lot to check my list of errands. A large van pulled up beside me, and a woman lowered her window asking me if she could see my van. Her disabled daughter, Renetta, was in her van, and they were looking for a smaller vehicle. She wondered if her daughter would fit into a van the size of ours. I opened the side door and lowered the lift. I told the woman her daughter was welcome to try our van out for size. We continued conversing for a short time and exchanged phone numbers. Just as the animals came two by two to Noah to board his lifesaving ark, God kept sending me people, and a support group began at our church.

God was telling me I needed to be obedient to Him no matter how inadequate I felt. He would take care of all the details. I identified with Moses when he was so hesitant to obey the Lord.

Working with disabled people would never have been my choice of ministries if it hadn't been for Kathryn. Until I experienced life with a handicapped child, I didn't know what to say to people in wheelchairs or parents of disabled children. I learned about empathy and saw firsthand how I could comfort others because I had suffered as II Corinthians 1:3–4 says. *"...the Father of mercies and God of all comfort, who comforts us in all our affliction, so that we may be able to comfort those who are in any affliction, with the comfort with which we ourselves are comforted by God."*

My aunt, a friend, and I were enjoying a cup of coffee and a piece of pie at Baker's Square when I noticed a mother with a child with some of Kathryn's features. As we were leaving the restaurant, I approached the woman and said, "Your daughter looks like she is doing really well."

There was no response from the mother. Her blank stare seemed to say, "Mind your own business. Don't patronize me. Leave me alone." Her response left me speechless! My simple comment, meant to be encouraging, created a terrible, hostile attitude. I was concerned about what to do next, but I shouldn't have feared. God gave me the right words. As calmly and quietly as I could, I said, "I hope my daughter will do as well as your daughter when she's her age."

Suddenly the woman's features went from angry to compassionate. "What's wrong with your daughter?" she asked.

"She has microcephaly, and she's one year old," I answered, matter of factly.

Quietly, with tears in her eyes she said, "That's what my daughter has. Her name is Julia. She's five years old."

Smiling, I said, "It's good to see she's doing so well. It encourages me, and I hope Kathryn will be as good when she is five."

The woman wished me well, and said she had enjoyed talking with me.

This mother was probably usually a likeable person, and maybe she'd had a bad day. Some people say hurtful things about disabled children, or point or stare rudely. She had possibly experienced unkindness in the past. Only God knows, but after our conversation, I felt certain that she trusted I knew all the emotions and feelings she had experienced the past five years. We were bonded by disability.

CHAPTER NINETEEN

By the time Kathryn was twelve, I was involved in teaching an ESL (English as a Second Language) outreach class to Japanese ladies at our church on Friday mornings. I wasn't sure I would be able to dedicate enough time to two different ministries. I prayed, asking God if I should continue the ESL classes or limit my ministry to the disabled. God showed me that these were not two separate ministries, but in so many ways, they were one.

In working with these Japanese ladies, I learned that even some modern Japanese people believe that having a disabled child means the mother of the child did something to anger her ancestors. The disabled child is her punishment. The guilt these Japanese mothers bear is horrendous!

After teaching the Japanese ladies for a couple of years, the coordinator of the Japanese ESL classes asked me to give my testimony. I eagerly agreed. I had second thoughts, though, when I told Rich that Mrs. Chiyozaki asked me to give my testimony. "She wants me to talk for thirty minutes. I don't know what I can share for that length of time."

Rich laughed, and with his usual good humor said, "Just pretend you have a telephone in your hand. You never have trouble talking on the phone that long." I didn't appreciate his sense of humor at the time. I worked all evening on my speech for the class. I presented the following speech with an interpreter and had no trouble filling the time.

My dad was an alcoholic. When I was a teenager he found out he had emphysema and was told he only had a year to live. We didn't have a lot of money, so he decided to gamble and "get rich quick" to leave his family better off. Instead of riches, he lost our home and all of our savings and moved to Arizona.

Three years after my mother, father and brothers moved to Arizona, my sister was diagnosed with a chemical imbalance and was in therapy for over a year before she got better.

My first marriage was a failure, and it ended in divorce. My ex-husband left me in an apartment with just a lawn chair to sleep on, my clothes and the pressure cooker I bought. I decided never to marry again, but God had different plans for my life.

God blessed me with a wonderful, loving caring husband, Rich. I was very happy when I found out that I was pregnant with our first child.

I felt so much guilt when my daughter, Kathryn, was born and we were told she wasn't going to live a week. I felt it must be my fault, and God was punishing me because He thought I was a bad person.

When my daughter was three years old, my older brother, Eddie, committed suicide. I felt that also was my fault.

I grew up in a religion that told me God was perfect.

If He was perfect, then He couldn't make mistakes. So all these things happening to me were not mistakes, but punishments. I believed that for many years.

As I spoke, I saw that the ladies were listening to every word I was saying. Some had tears in their eyes. I continued:

What finally freed me was asking Jesus into my heart as my personal savior. As I prayed and got closer to Jesus, He finally showed me He wasn't punishing me, but everything I went through in my life was allowed so I could draw closer to Him. God slowly took away my guilt as I read the Bible.

In John 9 it says, "And as He (Jesus) passed by, He saw a man blind from birth. And His disciples asked him, saying, 'Rabbi, who sinned, this man or his parents, that he should be born blind?' Jesus answered, 'It was neither that this man sinned, nor his parents; but it was in order that the works of God might be displayed in him.'"

God transformed my thinking. I knew He wasn't punishing me. God was going to use Kathryn and me to help other people with disabilities. He gave me Kathryn because parents of other disabled children would be able to relate to me. I finally had great peace about every part of my life.

I understand that in Japan disability is sometimes considered a curse from the ancestors. How awful for mothers of disabled children.

Every mother of a disabled child feels terrible guilt. I urge you to help these ladies when you get back to your home country. Make friends with Japanese mothers with disabled children. After all, disability can come to anyone at any age.

Most of the people in my disability group became disabled several years after they were born. Ecclesiastes 7:14 says, "Enjoy prosperity whenever you can, and when hard times come realize that God gives one as well as the other so that everyone will realize that nothing is certain in life." In other words, there are no guarantees in life. Just because a person is born healthy, it doesn't mean they will stay that way all of their lives. Your three-month-old child could wake up tomorrow morning with a high fever that doesn't go away. You take her to the doctor and she is diagnosed with an incurable disease. How would you feel? You have no control over the matter. Neither did the mom whose child was born sick.

God allows these things to happen so we put our dependency on Him, not ourselves. This prevents us from becoming prideful, but as we put our trust in God and seek to do His will, He reveals His plan and guides us through the hard times. Even after twenty years, my daughter has been the biggest blessing in my life, and I wouldn't trade her for the world. A mother doesn't love a disabled child less than a normal, healthy one. She just desperately needs the love and support of her family and close friends.

I then read them the following e-mail sent to me by Ellen Swanson, a friend from church.

"This story was written by a mother of a disabled child and it explains my feelings perfectly." I told the ladies.

WELCOME TO HOLLAND

By Emily Perl Kingsley
©1987 by Emily Perl Kingsley.
All rights reserved.
Reprinted by permission of the author.

I am often asked to describe the experience of raising a child with a disability—to try to help people who have not shared that unique experience to understand it, to imagine how it would feel. It's like this...

When you're going to have a baby, it's like planning a fabulous vacation trip—to Italy. You buy a bunch of guide books and make your wonderful plans. The Coliseum. The Michelangelo David. The gondolas in Venice. You may learn some handy phrases in Italian. It's all very exciting.

After months of eager anticipation, the day finally arrives. You pack your bags and off you go. Several hours later, the plane lands. The stewardess comes in and says, "Welcome to Holland."

"Holland?!!" you say. "What do you mean Holland?? I signed up for Italy! I'm supposed to be in Italy. All my life I've dreamed of going to Italy."

But there's been a change in the flight plan. They've landed in Holland and there you must stay.

The important thing is that they haven't taken you to a horrible, disgusting, filthy place, full of pestilence, famine and disease. It's just a different place.

So you must go out and buy new guide books. And

you must learn a whole new language. And you will meet a whole new group of people you would never have met.

It's just a *different* place. It's slower-paced than Italy, less flashy than Italy. But after you've been there for a while and you catch your breath, you look around...and you begin to notice that Holland has windmills...and Holland has tulips. Holland even has Rembrandts.

But everyone you know is busy coming and going from Italy...and they're all bragging about what a wonderful time they had there. And for the rest of your life, you will say "Yes, that's where I was supposed to go. That's what I had planned."

And the pain of that will never, ever, ever, ever go away...because the loss of that dream is a very, very significant loss.

But...if you spend your life mourning the fact that you didn't get to Italy, you may never be free to enjoy the very special, the very lovely things...about Holland.

My father always said, "Barb, if you have your health, you have everything." I used to believe that. But through the years I have seen very healthy people who were unhappy with their lives. My older brother was a good example of that. He had a doctor's degree in biology, a beautiful home in Texas, a beautiful wife, good job, nice cars, and lived comfortably. Yet he killed himself. Health, money and position don't bring you happiness. Only Jesus can do that.

As I started reading the Bible daily and asking God

to show me His plan for my life, only then did I have real peace in my heart and realize that God loves me more than anyone. He has taken away all my fears and has given me great joy in the midst of all my troubles. Jesus can help you with your struggles too.

After the class, several women came up to me to express how much they appreciated my testimony. Three of the ladies admitted that they had personal experiences similar to mine.

One told me, "My son has a glass eye. He was born with one eye missing. I have always been afraid my friends would find out and blame me. I don't tell people about his eye. Your talk made me feel better."

"Thank you. You have helped me more than I can say," said the second lady.

I never found out what she meant or how my talk could have helped her.

Another said, "I have a neighbor back in Japan with a disabled son. I have never talked to her or tried to be her friend. I feel ashamed of myself now. When I get back to Japan, I will be a good friend to her."

The speech went so well that three years later I was asked to share it again with a new ESL class. There was a similar response.

CHAPTER TWENTY

On a different occasion, a member of the Japanese church came to me after Sunday morning services and asked if she could talk to me. She was crying and seemed distressed. We found an empty room in the church, and there she told me she was pregnant.

I immediately responded with, "Congratulations!" It seemed an occasion to be overjoyed, but she was still very upset and cried even harder.

"You don't understand. I had an amniocentesis test and it showed that my baby will be born with Downs Syndrome. I feel ashamed and guilty because I thought of having an abortion."

Her news was shocking and I understood her concerns, but I tried not to show how surprised I was by her announcement. This fine woman helped me see more clearly how devastating a disability is to a Japanese family.

She continued, "My husband and I are going back to Japan in less than a year. My child would not have a good life in Japan. She would always be unacceptable in our culture."

My heart ached for her. She harbored so much guilt, and her child wasn't even born yet.

She continued, "I have been praying with a couple of my close church friends for God to show me what I should do. I know abortion is a sin and not acceptable for anyone, let alone a woman who professes to be a Christian. As I prayed, God pointed out Kathryn to me, and I see what a great gift she has been to you and Richard. I knew then I could not abort this child."

With tears streaming down my face, it was a while before I could respond. Finally, I could choke out a response. "The people in Japan, even some Christians, still believe that children like Kathryn are a curse. Maybe, just like the Old Testament story when God put Esther in the palace to save the Jews, He wants you to teach the Japanese people that every child, even a disabled one, is a gift from Him. Can you imagine what great things you can do to free mothers in Japan from the guilt of what is considered a curse? You know it's not a curse. God doesn't make mistakes and He has a special plan for your baby and for you."

My friend's face told me she was going to be doing some praying about what we had discussed. Eventually, she did return to Japan. When opportunities arise, she shares her story with mothers who have special needs kids. But there is an interesting twist to this story. The amniocentesis test was wrong. Her daughter was born perfectly healthy; she did not have Downs Syndrome. God used Kathryn to save one little girl's life.

I firmly believe that God blessed her for her obedience. Though she may never have known she aborted a perfectly healthy daughter, she may have experienced tremendous guilt. Most of all, she would also have missed out on one of God's biggest blessings...her daughter.

CHAPTER TWENTY-ONE

Kathryn has touched the lives of many people. We probably won't know how many until we get to heaven, but with each time I learn of another example of someone being inspired or comforted or encouraged by our daughter, I see how one small girl can influence and touch lives.

My husband's niece, Carrie, had to write an essay for school about something they did over summer break. Here are her own words:

Hello, my name is Carrie Christopher. I am ten years old and in the fifth grade. My topic is Misericordia Home.

I am a volunteer for Misericordia. This is a home for mentally retarded children. What does the name Misericordia mean? It's a French word meaning "Heart of Mercy." I worked for Sister Rosemary Connelly, who is the Administrator and one of my favorite people.

This is how I spent my summer, some of it anyway. I have been very much involved with Misericordia Home. This summer we had a festival in order to raise money for a dream of Sister Rosemary's; to build a city for these wonderful children. Where do these children go as age slowly creeps upon them? Back home to mom and dad, who in some cases are dead? Well Sister Rosemary had an "idea." Let's build a city for these adults who can live a near normal adult life. We even received free advertisement from Channel 5. This time was donated so Sister Rosemary's ideas can be brought to television viewers.

We have many other volunteers who donated their time, not only to the children, but who participate in fundraising. My job at the festival was in the children's games. I helped them create crafts. I also took care of the younger children. That day, through ads, prizes and the selling of many items (which by the way, were donated by the people), we were a great success. We hope this summer will surpass last summer because now we are becoming nationally known.

Now you're probably wondering how my mom and I got involved with Misericordia? I have a cousin, who if God wills her to live to be my age, will never see, walk, talk or be able to think. This is the reason I am involved.

I thank the Lord for helping me to understand this way of life.

It takes much love and compassion and I feel a better person for doing this. Perhaps, if you should hear about us this summer, you will remember this and that would be GREAT.

When my niece, Carrie, grew up, she chose nursing as her career. She worked at Children's Memorial Hospital on the children's oncology ward. She is now a wonderful mother to three boys, Jackson, Matthew, and Lucas, and a girl, Ava Kathryn.

Ava's middle name was in honor of our daughter Kathryn. This sweet gesture shows that Carrie is as sensitive today as she was at age ten when she wrote this beautiful tribute to her cousin, our daughter.

CHAPTER TWENTY-TWO

God has put many caring, sensitive people into my life since April 3, 1979. Support came from many different sources and in different ways. I am blessed to be in a church family that really cares about Rich, Kathryn, and me. The people there accepted Kathryn from the first day we attended.

On June 24, 1997, David West, a young man in our church, handed me this poem that he had written for Kathryn.

A GIFT FROM GOD

Take comfort, Kathryn, in all your cries,
Not one tear fell without God's watchful eyes.
Sunday morning, Jesus stopped me from walking by,
I was blessed as I saw Christ's reflection in your beautiful blue eyes.

You touched my heart so deeply as I saw you sitting there,
I was overwhelmed to hug you, and pull you from your chair.
As tears of joy ran down my face, I said, "Lord, what do I say?"
No ample words could I speak, how blessed I felt that day.

Kathryn, blessings come in many ways, and you are surely one.
As it was to me I pray, that you would know God's Son.

Thank you, Kathryn, for what you said as I came walking near,
"Don't walk by me, I'm God's child too, talk to me, I'll hear."

The amazing work God gets done when he has a special tool,
To work in lives like mine, to know such a special jewel.
So Kathryn, whatever life brings, you know you can afford.
In your own special way, make a joyful noise unto the Lord.

To Mom and Dad Blasco, I pray you'll always see,
The precious gift of Kathryn, that is surely heavenly.

This will always be a precious gift from David to me. He gave it to me on a day when I needed encouragement. Besides applying to my own struggles with Kathryn, my cousin Sue's little son, Tommy, not quite two years old, was losing his battle with leukemia, and I was really down in the dumps that day.

As I read this poem, I wondered if Kathryn would ever understand who Jesus was and what He did for her. As the years went by, I saw that she did know Jesus. She may not comprehend the full story of His birth, ministry, death, and resurrection, but she certainly responds to His name. She gets excited and reaches out for my hand so she can shake it vigorously. She listens intently as Rich and I read Scripture to her. When she hears the name of Jesus, she has a big smile on her face.

CHAPTER TWENTY-THREE

Another friend, Ruth Martindale, wrote this poem about Kathryn. Writing poems was her hobby. Many have been published through the years.

KATHRYN

I wasn't the normal baby
So long anticipated.
I wasn't the healthy child
So eagerly awaited.

Born with a damaged brain
And eyes that could not see,
My parents sadly questioned
Why God should give them me!

But when they accepted Jesus
They saw with different eyes,
That my birth was for a reason,
And a blessing in disguise!

My gentle disposition
And the way I often smile,
Has brought my parents joy
And made everything worthwhile!

And their tender love for me
Now has overlapped,
To reaching out to parents
Of other handicapped.

Now they understand why
God in His good pleasure,
Gave them, though handicapped,
A most very special treasure!

There were others who expressed to me how much Kathryn had impacted their lives. My cousin Greg's daughter, Shannon, told me about a school assignment to write about someone who made a great impression on her. She said she wrote an essay about Kathryn, and she got an "A" on her paper. Shannon, like Carrie, is growing up to be a loving, sensitive young lady.

One Sunday morning in 2007, a woman came up to me at church. Her words cheered me. "I'm so glad you bring your daughter to church. My two-year-old son loves to touch her. When he does that, she gives him a big smile."

I said, "Thank you for sharing that."

"No, thank you. I know your daughter's presence is making an impact on our children. As they get older, they won't be afraid to be around disabled people or talk to them."

Steve Smith, a father of two young daughters, came up to me at Kathryn's 30th birthday party at church. He said, "I just have to tell you how much Kathryn has impacted my two daughter's lives. They grew up in the church with her and today they don't see her wheelchair or her disability, they just see Kathryn the person."

What they both said was true. If children are exposed to disabled people at a young age, they will not feel awkward when they see or meet them. This is obvious in the siblings of disabled children.

If God has a plan for each of our lives, and I believe He does, He has a plan for Kathryn's life also. The sensitivity others have developed because of the impact Kathryn has had on their lives is part of God's great plan for Kathryn. She has touched many lives, in many different ways. She can't talk nor walk, but God is using her just as she is.

On the other hand, I'm sure that some people have been turned off by Kathryn's presence at church. Her unusual, loud noises, sometimes in an area where people in the congregation can hear, are certainly a distraction. They can be very unnerving to older people, not used to loud, unexpected sounds. I pray that if a new or unfamiliar person is in the audience, it won't make their first exposure to our church a negative experience. If they investigate, they will see who is making the noise and why. This can be a witnessing opportunity for Rich and me, and it can be a growing experience for them. I know that God takes such situations and turns them into something good that will be glorifying to Him.

Another young disabled girl in our church, Katie, responds out loud to the rhetorical questions sometimes asked by Pastor Manny in his sermons. This could be an annoyance, but it has been turned into a positive situation. Katie's mom, Cheryl, told us that several people have come up to her after the service and said, "Katie is a real example to me. She puts me to shame. She really listens to the sermon and doesn't get distracted as I sometimes do. I have to learn to listen better they way she does."

From what we've heard from people in our church, more positive than negative has been the result of Katie's and Kathryn's attendance at our church.

Our wedding day, April 9, 1978.

Kathryn came home from the hospital
on Christmas Eve, one week after
her head surgery.

Swimming with the help of mom at five months old.
Doing it alone a couple of years later.

A visit with 'Grandma' Kay in California at five months old.

I quit sucking my thumb a long time ago.

At age two, Kathryn is in the 0-3 year old program.

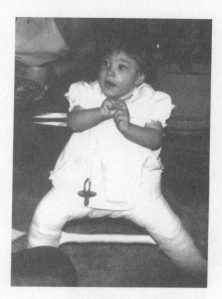

Kathryn celebrated her third birthday
in a full body cast after her first hip
surgery in March, 1982.

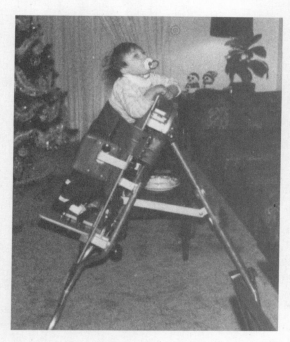

At age three, Kathryn got a new prone stander just
in time for Christmas.

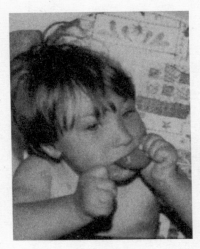

Kathryn quickly learned to feed
herself the foods she loved.

Carrie and Kathryn at the Caring
Parents Organization Support
Group's Easter Pancake Breakfast
in 1983.

Kathryn starts private therapy
at home with Laura.

By age five, Kathryn had already learned to get into a sitting position all by herself.

How about a side view this time, Mom?

Dressing up for Halloween at Julia Molloy was a big event. Dig them cowboy boots!

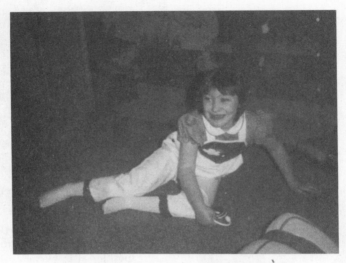

This was one of the last times that Kathryn would sit independently. Her last hip surgery, at age ten, took away her ability to get into a sitting position all by herself.

Hurry up and take this picture Mom, so we can go to the birthday party.

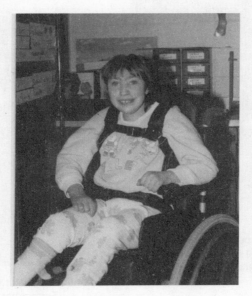

Kathryn at Julia Molloy at age twelve.

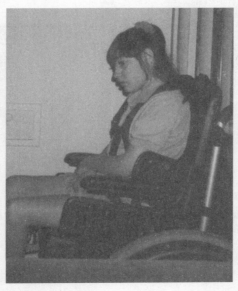

Kathryn at age twenty-one now attending
Shore, an adult day care center.

My grandmother, with only one year of formal schooling, created a small financial dynasty.

Mom and Dad's wedding day, September 7, 1940.

My sister Pat at brother Jim's second wedding in Arizona 1985.

My older brother, Eddie with his wife Helen in 1976, five years before he committed suicide.

My younger brother, Jimmy, and me at cousin
Greg's wedding July 10, 1982.

My Aunt Bernice, Uncle Chester, and cousins Sue, Greg, and Tom
at cousin Debbie's wedding 0ctober 7, 1989. Her husband John
died nine months later on July 4, 1990 from heart disease.

Dennis and Georgette Syverson.
Dennis repaired my car,
Georgette repaired my
relationship with God.

Helen Slusarz, my marital matchmaker.
Thank you for introducing me to Richard!

Cate and Bob Fink, Kathryn's guardian angels and our gift from God.

Joni Eareckson Tada's visit kicking off the newly established
H.I.M. (Hearts in Motion) Disability Ministry at Glenview
Evangelical Free Church.

Kathryn with her volunteer Becky Thornburgh and JAF
Staffer, Rita Houston, at the 2009 JAF Family Retreat in
Muskegon, Michigan.

PART FIVE

The Lessons

Be strong and courageous, do not be afraid

or tremble at them, for the Lord your

God is the one who goes with you.

He will not leave you nor forsake you.

DEUTERONOMY 31:6

No one with a disabled child can go through the experiences of parenting that child without earning a Master's Degree in Disability. I've learned many lessons in Kathryn's thirty years of life. I always tell people that my daughter taught me more in her first five years of life than I could have taught her in her whole lifetime. It is my desire to share this knowledge with others so they might not experience the hurt and heartache I have endured at times.

1) Don't judge others.

The day after Kathryn came home from the hospital, I was holding her and listening to the Phil Donahue Show. Phil's guest that day was Mrs. Quinlan, who was telling her side of the story about her daughter.

In April of 1975, at twenty-one, Mrs. Quinlan's daughter, Karen, overdosed by consuming alcohol and tranquilizers at a party. Doctors saved her life, but her brain was damaged and she went into a coma. The doctors placed her on life support, and Karen lived for several months in a vegetative state. The Quinlans were the first people who tried to get their daughter off the life-support machine. The media called it "pulling the plug." The doctors were against taking Karen off the ventilator, so her parents went to court. This was the first time someone challenged the medical field regarding life-support machines, so it got a lot of publicity both in the newspaper and on television. Public opinion seemed to weigh heavily against the Quinlans. I remember myself thinking, "What kind of a mother would take her daughter off of the machine and let her die?"

However, that morning in 1979, I wept as I listened to Mrs. Quinlan tell her side of the story that had ravaged their lives four years earlier. She was in tears as she relayed all the details of the trial. "People walked past my house and yelled obscenities at me and my husband. Some people even threw bricks through our windows. Making this decision was the hardest thing we had to do. Seeing Karen lying in that hospital room day after day not responding to anyone or anything and getting awful bed sores was more than a mother can bear."

My heart broke for the Quinlans. Just hours earlier as I held Kathryn, I prayed that if she couldn't have a normal, healthy life, God would take her. I couldn't imagine my daughter living the life described to us by the doctors, "a vegetable laying in the fetal position the rest of her life." Right after I prayed, I was filled with guilt. What kind of a mother am I? What mother would pray that her child would die?

When I first heard the Karen Quinlan story on television, I threw "verbal bricks" at Mrs. Quinlan also. Certainly, I was no better than the others who threw real bricks through their windows. Was the Lord telling me "Don't judge anyone until you have walked in their shoes?" Ironically, years later, Mrs. Quinlan was teaching me that these thoughts and feelings about my daughter were normal. In this, Mrs. Quinlan and I were alike. Every mother wants the best for her children.

The Quinlan's story was not over after the judge ruled for the parents to "pull the plug" on their daughter. Instead of dying within a short time, Karen Quinlan began breathing on her own and lived in a nursing home for ten more years until 1985. She died of pneumonia.

I used Karen's illustration when I counseled with a referral mom at Lutheran General Hospital a year later. God, not man, is in control of our lives. He determines life and death. Only He can "pull the plug," and it will be in His time and His way.

Through the years, Rich and I experienced our share of being judged. Several years ago, we went to a small drive up, fast food restaurant to get dinner. It was a beautiful summer day, not hot, not cold, just a perfect temperature. We decided to leave Kathryn in the van, order our dinner, and eat at an outside table close to where the van was parked. This restaurant had large windows all the way around, so even inside the restaurant we could see Kathryn.

As I was standing in line deciding what to order, a very upset lady walked into the restaurant screaming, "Who left that poor, helpless child in that van? She is crying, and no one is around to take care of her."

I knew she was referring to Kathryn and spoke up. "That's our daughter, and she's okay. She makes those screeching sounds because she hears cars driving by and people talking. She is legally blind, noises stimulate her, and she responds by making loud sounds." I tried to explain Kathryn's condition so the concerned woman would know that she wasn't distressed and in need of help, but she was beyond seeing our side of what she thought was child neglect. I couldn't get my point across.

The woman was anything but calm. "You're an unfit mother and should be arrested," she yelled at me.

I don't take scolding lying down, so I tried again. "You don't understand. Even if my daughter were right here next to us, she would still be making those sounds for the same reason. She's over-stimulated."

The woman walked out of the restaurant in a huff, yelling obscenities at me. Needless to say, we had the attention of every-one in the restaurant.

On the way home, I was furious. I spewed at Richard. "Who is that woman to judge me? She doesn't know me. She wasn't there when I nursed Kathryn back to health after five surgeries. She wasn't there all those nights when I slept in a chair next to her hospital bed. Where was she when I ran from hospital to hospital trying to find out more about her condition? And what about when I had to take her to the doctor every week for the first year of her life? She wasn't there then, either. How can she judge me?" I went on and on, angry that a total stranger had the gall to say such horrible things to me.

I calmed down, and when I was rational again, I knew and understood why she judged me. She didn't know me. She didn't want my explanation. If I gave her the benefit of the doubt, pos-sibly she was embarrassed because she made such a snap deci-sion without knowing or hearing my side of the story. I knew my daughter was safe in the van. There was no way that she could hurt herself. We could see her from where we were standing. This woman's reaction made us realize that sometimes people don't see things the same way we do.

After this incident, I found myself continually explaining to people why I do certain things. For instance, when we take Kathryn to a party or church where there are a lot of people, we sometimes put her off in a corner or in another room where we can see her, but where she is away from the crowd. When she is in the midst of the crowd, she gets loud and upset. When she's upset, her schedule gets upset also.

Though we're sensitive to Kathryn's noises, other people often understand she is not in distress and reassure us. Hearing, "Don't worry! Kathryn's sounds don't bother us. Bring her here," helps us feel comfortable having her out with us.

If we're among strangers, a short explanation clears matters. Either Rich or I will say, "The main reason we don't want Kathryn close by is because she gets over-stimulated. When she gets over-stimulated she can't sleep at night, and then her sleep is turned around for several days until she gets back on schedule. When she is away from the crowd it's for her protection, not because we're ashamed of her sounds."

People are also interested in Kathryn's eating habits. We usually feed her before we go somewhere, even if it is to a place where we will be eating. There are several reasons. She is a picky eater. At home, we can feed her foods she likes. She often won't eat in or near a crowd because she is over-stimulated. Our friends often ask, "Aren't you going to feed Kathryn?"

Most of the time, I tell them she's already eaten, but sometimes after several people have asked me the same question I make a joke about it. "Oh, no, not today! We have her on a strict diet this week."

I understand how people would think we aren't giving Kathryn the attention or care she requires. Some parents of disabled children might feel they don't owe anyone an explanation. I feel I'm not so much explaining why I do something to justify my action, but educating people about the reasons I do what I do. Whatever we do, it's what's best for Kathryn.

2) Don't avoid questions about your disabled child; use this opportunity to educate others.

One day, when Kathryn was about two years old, I took her to the bakery with me. I was holding her on my shoulder and I couldn't see her face. I didn't know that her bonnet had come down a little and was covering her eyes. A woman in the bakery noticed and said, "Your daughter's bonnet is covering her eyes; she can't see anything." Her voice was curt.

I tried the simple but direct approach. "Thank you, but she's blind, so she can't see anything anyway," I replied. My simple reply backfired on me.

"How was I to know that?" she said and walked off angrily.

I wondered if I should have given her less information and just said, "Thank you." I realized later that the woman was perfectly comfortable talking to me when she thought that Kathryn was "normal." When she realized she was disabled, her whole demeanor changed. After that experience, I learned to weigh my words more carefully.

Children sometimes react to Kathryn better than some adults do. They ask questions that adults wish they had the nerve to ask. When we went to Rich's niece's graduation party, I was sitting by a table holding Kathryn. She was about five years old, but very small for her age.

While at Carrie's graduation party, a little boy walked over to talk to me. He nodded toward Kathryn and our simple conversation went something like this:

"What's her name?"

"Kathryn."

"How old is she?"

"She's five years old."

"Why is she sitting on your lap? Can she come and play with me?"

"No, I'm sorry. Kathryn doesn't walk or talk. She won't be able to play with you."

"Why can't she walk?"

"She was born sick."

"Oh. Will she get better?"

"No, she will be this way the rest of her life."

Often, children worry that Kathryn can't do everything they can. This boy was no different. He wasn't finished. His next question was fully expected. They all ask it. "Will she be able to go to school?"

"She does go to school. It's a special school for children like Kathryn that can't walk or talk."

We continued chatting for several more minutes. His mother, in earshot of the conversation, was getting uncomfortable. She fidgeted. She intervened. "Honey, that's enough 'Twenty Questions.' Why don't you go outside and play with the other kids."

He obeyed his mother, but added to me, "I hope Kathryn will get better."

As he scooted out the door, I told the mom I wasn't uncomfortable with all his questions. A child learns from his curiosity.

Once, when I took Kathryn to Sears, another boy approached us. I was looking at costume jewelry and didn't notice him right away.

Curiously, the boy asked, 'How come she's in that chair?"

"She can't walk," I answered.

"How come she can't walk?"

I try to keep my explanations straightforward with children, so I said, "She can't walk because she can't see."

He thought about that for a moment before his final comment that left me in stitches. "She can't see? So where's her dog?"

I said, "She doesn't walk, so she doesn't need a guide dog."

The boy's face fell and he said with concern, "Now I'm really depressed." He walked away sadly.

I chuckled to myself and couldn't wait to get home and call Rich at work. This boy tickled my funny bone and, in his innocent way, made my day.

When Kathryn was about fifteen years old, we had company over for dinner when the phone rang. I answered the telephone.

"Is Kathryn there?" the young man at the other end asked.

"Yes, she is," I answered, surprised that our daughter was getting a phone call.

The young man said, "I want to talk to her."

I said, "I'm sorry, but Kathryn doesn't talk. Who is this?"

The boy said, "I go to school with her. How come she can't talk?"

"She doesn't know how to talk."

He was insistent, "Let me talk to Kathryn."

I was equally determined to get my point across. "Honey, I told you she doesn't know how to talk."

Deflated, he responded, "Oh, forget it. I'll call someone else."

I went back into the dining room and said, "I think I just botched Kathryn's first date. I wonder if she'll ever forgive me."

Many people have a hard time knowing what to say when they encounter Kathryn. I was in their shoes before our daughter was born, uncomfortable around disabled people. Most of the time, I find that being open and honest is best, but sometimes it isn't. One of the lessons I've learned is that not everyone is the same. What is helpful and appropriate information for one person is not for another.

3) Don't misinterpret other people's words or actions.

Having good hearing is not always a blessing. At times, I've wished my hearing was not quite so acute. We took Kathryn to Disney World when she was ten years old. I went into a store and Rich stayed by the inside door with Kathryn. I found what I needed and went to check out. As I was in line, there were two women behind me talking. All of a sudden, Kathryn made one of her loud happy sounds and the two women noticed.

"Isn't that sad?" the first woman asked.

"Yes, and there are so many of them here," the other one replied.

I wasn't sure just how they meant that, but their voices didn't sound mean. I wanted to turn around and say, "That's my daughter. She's a very happy girl, and she has a great life. She has been the biggest blessing in our lives. Please don't feel bad for her." I didn't say anything, however. I knew that they would be embarrassed if they knew I was her mother and overheard their conversation. Less said this time was definitely better.

4) Good will come out of a bad situation if you surrender to God's will.

Often, the reason it's not easy to approach a disabled person is because people feel sorry for them and their family because they don't meet the standards set by society, they don't look like the rest of society, and they don't act like everyone else. I often felt the same way before Kathryn was born and when she was little. I was afraid that I would say the wrong thing and hurt someone's feelings.

When she was first born, I prayed that Kathryn would live

for one milestone or another, but I also prayed that she wouldn't live many times, and I felt it was an unselfish prayer. I reasoned, what kind of life would it be, stuck in a wheelchair? She would never go to college, get married, or give us grandchildren. As each of her five surgeries came and went, I prayed. "Please, Lord, take her away from this life of pain." As it turned out, in a way, He did take her away from pain. After each surgery, Kathryn would come out smiling. If she had any pain, it wasn't noticeable. God knew we needed His comfort. Since all of her surgeries when she was so young, Kathryn has been very healthy. She hasn't had a cold in over ten years. Once when I got the flu, she caught it. I had it for seven days. She was herself the next day. I am thankful that her immune system seems to work better than most.

As the years have gone by, I see that Kathryn's life does have meaning and purpose. Our church has become involved in disability ministry. Our H.I.M. Ministry has a generous budget. Families that never could afford a vacation because of medical expenses are being sent to weeklong retreats organized by Joni and Friends. Our church has sponsored families to attend these get-away summer vacations each year for the past ten years. When the families return after a rejuvenating week, they send thank you notes saying how much fun they had and how wonderful it was to be around people who understood and shared their pain. One grateful mom wrote, "It was the best week of my life since my daughter became disabled. We could never have afforded that vacation on our own. But the best part was spending part of the day away from our daughter and being able to share concerns with other parents in the same position. We learned a lot. The only bad part of the whole vacation was that we had to come home, back to the real world."

With funds and help from church and Joni and Friends,

house ramps have been built for those who need and request them. One mother called asking for a lift for her van. Our church paid for half and Joni and Friends' Matching Funds Program paid the other half.

While at a Joni and Friends Family Retreat, volunteer Marge Hatter had an opportunity to talk with many families. She learned that there were many disabled people who needed medical equipment which was not available through or provided by insurance companies. Being a nurse, she knew that there were people who had medical equipment from a loved one who had either passed away or outgrown the equipment. Many of these items were no longer being used and were being stored in garages or attics. She had a brilliant idea. Using e-mail, she started *The Medical Equipment Connection,* a purely goodwill effort, not part of any not-for-profit organization. People contact her if they need equipment, or if they have equipment that they want to give away or sell. Marge connects people who have needs with those who have surpluses. Our H.I.M. ministry often locates equipment that Marge is able to put on her website. If Wheels for the World (Joni and Friends) cannot use something, Marge can. Wheels for the World does not accept electric wheelchairs, ramps, portable potties, or bathtub chairs. These items cannot be shipped overseas for handicapped people in other countries, so many are put on Marge's *Medical Equipment Connection,* which provides the contacts for the exchanges. This connection has been a blessing to hundreds of needy people.

Frank Tessien, a Boy Scout from our church, wanted his Eagle Scout project to involve disabled people and asked if our Hearts in Motion ministry and I would help him. I suggested that he organize a wheelchair drive for Joni and Friends' Wheels for the World. It was H.I.M.'s first and most successful drive.

Frank filled his grandmother's empty garage from floor to ceiling with wheelchairs, canes, crutches, and walkers. Joni and Friends sent them to prisons where inmates repaired and refurbished the wheelchairs. Then the chairs were distributed to disabled people in underprivileged countries all over the world. Richard and I continue with this project collecting equipment and delivering it to Joni and Friends several times each year. Truckloads have been sent from the Chicago area worldwide to disabled people since Frank's first project!

A few years later, Jonathan Huffman, another Boy Scout in our church wanted to do a project aimed at helping the disabled. At that time, Joni and Friends was offering free computers to disabled people, but when I asked people in my support group if they wanted them, they said, "No." I later learned they didn't want them because they didn't know how to use a computer. After learning that this was a concern, Jonathan designed his Eagle Scout project to go beyond acquiring free computers. He attained five computers from Joni and Friends, found five people willing to learn how to use them, and five instructors willing to teach the disabled. Lessons were given on accessing e-mail and the internet and using a word document so they could write letters. Jonathan supervised the program.

I was thrilled when both Frank and Jonathan received their Eagle Scout awards and asked Rich and me to come to their presentation ceremonies.

Another Joni and Friends program that has attracted interest from people in our church and encouraged their involvement in Hearts in Motion is called "Special Delivery." During the Christmas season, Joni and Friends sent several boxes of books, musical tapes for adults and children, large-print Bibles, Joni's hand painted Christmas cards, etc.

The H.I.M. Ministry purchased gift cards, chocolates and ornaments, and we made up gift bags for people in our support group. Around the second week of December, we took a group of church members caroling at homes of the disabled. We hand delivered the Special Delivery packages. One year, a church member, Don Skoglund, made the trip even more special. He brought his accordion and played on the bus as we all sang and had a great time. Shortly after Christmas, I found out how sick Don was on that trip. He had liver cancer and his wife, Shirley, told me later that he was in pain but insisted that he go. His passing a few months later saddened our church family. The dedication of the volunteers involved with our H.I.M. group is amazing.

The following year we had two more musicians from church accompany us to make our special deliveries. Bud Swanson came with his accordion and brought his eight-year-old son, Luke, who was learning to play the viola. As we arrived at each person's home, Bud played and we sang. After a couple of songs, Bud turned to Luke and said, "What song would you like to play for us?" Luke answered, "O Little Town of Bethlehem." At each home, his response was the same that evening. Bud confided to me on the way home that Luke didn't know any other Christmas songs. He had learned this one song so he could participate in a special way.

When our old church van broke down, we changed our delivery service. We called it "One Hour for Jesus." Individuals in the church would pick up a package and deliver it. They would spend a few minutes with each family to get to know them better. Each delivery person said it was a great way to begin the Christmas season.

As the years went by, our Special Delivery expanded to our church's Nursing Home Ministry which involves five nursing homes in our community. At each of these homes, volunteers lead Sunday morning services. Teams sing, lead music, and preach a short message. The organizer of this ministry asked me if we could give these gift packages to the nursing home clients. The first year, our choir director, Robin Olen, organized the children's choir, and they sang at each nursing home. As they finished singing, the children handed gift bags to each of the people. These elderly people were thrilled, but they were more grateful to see the smiling faces of the young children.

5) Life does not come with a guarantee.

Just looking at my two friends' lives, Abbie and her sister, Jo, should speak volumes to us that there are no guarantees in life. Little did we know when Abbie came to visit me for the first time after my daughter's birth that Kathryn would outlive her. Abbie was diagnosed with multiple sclerosis a few years later. At first, the illness was undetectable, but slowly it began to drain the life from her. It progressed through its usual stages: first, she needed to use a walker, then a manual wheelchair until she needed a motorized one, and after four years of bed confinement, she died in December of 2007. It was hard for me to see Abbie wither away like that. Having experienced our pain, we were able to share hers.

Abbie and I had been friends for two months. She was my co-worker at Dynascan when we met in 1977. She was bright, vivacious, and happy, with a great sense of humor. She was kind to me. As our friendship grew, I confided in her about my divorce and financial situation.

I came to work one day, and the air-conditioning was on high. It was obvious to Abbie that I was cold. "Where's your sweater?" she asked.

I dismissed her concern saying, "I don't have one. I'll get by until payday, then I can go buy one."

The very next day, Abbie brought me a sweater she purchased on the way home the night before. It was no surprise to anyone when we became best friends. I was proud to have her stand up with me on my wedding day the following year.

Abbie wanted desperately to get pregnant. She had been married for several years and unable to conceive. She and Tom were contemplating adoption, so I was excited when she announced at our wedding rehearsal, "I'm pregnant. Hurry up and get pregnant, too, so we can go to the zoo together with our kids."

With all of this in mind when Abbie first visited Kathryn and me, I wanted to assure my friend that though I hurt about our baby, I was overjoyed that she and Tom had their new infant daughter, Heather. She had been born just four months earlier, healthy and strong.

Abbie's illness was physically and emotionally difficult. Many of her friends stopped visiting after her speech became indistinguishable. I could understand that. At times, it was hard for me to know what she was saying also, but I knew how important it was to both of us that we maintain our relationship.

Jo Guza, Abbie's sister, had the same problem when Abbie's speaking became difficult to understand, however, she still came faithfully to care for her sister. As Abbie's swallowing became affected by her illness, Jo often prepared foods that were easier for Abbie to eat. In the early stages of Abbie's MS, the three of us played pinochle together, but as Abbie's health failed more and more, Jo and I could only visit at her bedside.

Jo's life didn't come with guarantees, either. Years before Abbie was diagnosed with MS, Jo's daughter Angela died from kidney cancer. The doctors told Jo that her daughter was born with this cancer. After several years of treatments, it looked as if Angela was going to beat the disease, but the cancer returned and took her life. One week before she was supposed to make her First Communion in the Catholic Church, at the age of eight, Angela was buried in her communion dress.

After burying her daughter, Jo was angry with God. She vowed she would never go to church again, and would certainly never go to anyone's First Communion service. Time would heal her, but at that point, her pain and anger was intense, sharp, and real. A couple years later, our Kathryn was going to make her First Communion with her class of special-needs children. She and a group of handicapped kids learned about Jesus and His love in creative ways. I was excited to see our daughter participate in this milestone in her life and invited everyone to the service and lun-cheon following, Jo included. Jo came to the church. Afterwards, however, I saw her head for the door and ran to ask her to join us at our home for the party.

With tears in her eyes, she answered me, "I can't. I have to leave."

I was concerned for Jo the rest of the day. I couldn't imagine what happened. Why was she so upset? Did someone do or say something to her I didn't know about? The next day I called to talk to her.

Our conversation was enlightening. I had been so absorbed with Kathryn's surgeries taking my time, energy, and effort, I never knew the entire story of Angela's death and First Communion. After our talk, I realized the only reason she came to Kathryn's service was because she knew how important it was to me. Only a person who had gone through what she experienced could relate to another hurting person as she had done for me. I loved her even more for her sacrifice and love. Our friendship grew stronger and we became like family.

Jo's anger remained for years. Healing began when her third son, Timmy, was born, a couple years after Angela's death. She still hadn't gone back to church or completely forgiven God. Possibly, it was her way of progressing through grieving. I was confused, though. She collected angels to remind her of Angela. I wondered how she could believe in angels and not God.

Jo's husband Paul suffered a heart attack several years later. With quick thinking and CPR, Jo saved his life. He did well for several years after that. Then all the stress in her life took a toll on her health, and she suffered a stroke. Thankfully, it was mild, and after months of therapy, it was hardly noticeable that she had been sick.

Once after she came home from the hospital, Rich and I went to visit. She still couldn't speak clearly. Her mouth was having trouble saying the words her head was thinking. She desperately tried to tell me something.

"I better, I tell you Frafrin."

"Are you trying to tell me that when you get better there is something you want to tell me about Kathryn?" I translated what she said.

"Yes," came out with a vigorous nod.

Recovering after much therapy, Jo was able to tell me she understood Kathryn better. She believed Kathryn was as she had been during her stroke. She understood everything we were saying, but she couldn't express herself verbally, a frustrating condition.

As I began to observe Kathryn more carefully, I believe now that part of what Jo said was true. I'm not sure that Kathryn comprehends everything that we say, but she surely understands a lot more than we gave her credit for.

Jo's husband Paul died of cancer a few years later, causing another void in her life.

I'm sure there is a big part of her that wishes life would have turned out differently, but her children, grandchildren, and looking after her widowed aunt, keep her busy and keep her life full.

Some people seem to go through more trials than others. I believe trials are God's way of getting our attention and that all trials in life serve a greater purpose.

I like the way Job viewed life. He had lost his sons and daughters, all his cattle, sheep, oxen, and camels. He was terribly afflicted with horrible sores all over his body. He was not even recognizable when his friends came to comfort him. His wife in her compassion for him thought he would be better off dead. "Why don't you curse God and die?" she asked. Job looked at her and shook his head. "Oh foolish woman, do we accept good from God and not trouble?" Job knew that God's loving discipline molds and shapes our lives so we become what God sees we are capable of being. He knows far better than we do what great potential there is in our suffering to transform our messed up view of life into a life of godly service.

We don't know what road God will lead us down to attain His purpose for our life. As Kathryn grows older, I find myself working with more parents of disabled children. Though a child is born healthy, he or she may develop a disability later. Several people in our support group have become disabled through illness or an accident. Many of these are not children, but adults who led productive lives up to that point.

In our opinion, these parents and children have it much harder than Kathryn, Rich, and me. Rich and I knew from her birth that Kathryn was going to be severely retarded and multi-handicapped. Doctors assured us she wasn't going to live long, so we did not build up hopes or expectations. We strive to do as much as possible to give our daughter love and as much caring as we can. Our goal is to see that her world is comfortable and safe and that she is content.

Kathryn is content and happy in the small, protected world she knows. There is no comprehension that she is different; this is the life she's always known. However, for parents and families in which a child gets sick or injured after being healthy and normal, it is harder. Prior to the disability, parents and siblings experienced a "normal" child, walking, talking, playing, growing, and developing. All of a sudden, these activities end. A whole new set of daily routines and behaviors takes the place of things that were taken for granted. It is a devastating new world suddenly thrust upon the family.

These disappointments and frustrations are obviously noticeable for the family members of the disabled person. The child or adult has had everything stripped away. They knew and experienced a different, independent life, and then they find themselves suddenly dependent upon others, disabled and handicapped. Many go through terrible depression until finally coming to grips with reality and accepting their new situation. Some never reach this level of acceptance. Life is more complicated and difficult for such people and their families.

This was Joni Eareckson Tada's story after a diving accident at age eighteen left her a quadriplegic. The devastation she felt almost destroyed her will to live until she discovered that God had a big plan for her life. He turned her horrible accident into a worldwide ministry addressing the needs of other disabled people. After coping with her paralysis, she started her organization Joni and Friends. She has become an outspoken voice and advocate for disabled people in Washington, D.C., and all over the world.

Her ministry includes radio and television programs, and she has authored over seventy books. In her autobiography, *Joni*, she talks about her accident and how she struggled until she finally overcame her fears. The book was made into a movie a couple of years later. Joni is a talented artist painting with her mouth, and has a beautiful singing voice. She gives motivational speeches all over the country, and she has travelled to 105 depressed countries, delivering medical equipment where none is available. When she was leaving the hospital after her accident and many months of rehabilitation, her nurse told her, "Joni, do all that you can do with what you have left to do it with." Joni has certainly exceeded any expectation this nurse had in mind for her. After forty-two years in a wheelchair, she is still serving the Lord with every ounce of energy she has left. If you asked her how she is able to do all that she does, she would answer, "My strength is in the Lord."

Parents of adult-onset disability must deal with more problems. When Kathryn was born, we immediately began working with the hospital support team. There were already school systems in place for her. When a child or adult becomes disabled after birth at any age, the parents of this child are typically on their own to find out what is available for their newly disabled dependent. The hope is that their hospital has a good support system that can take them through the maze of personnel and agencies available. Unless they get into a support group, or connect with other parents who have gone through a similar experience, they are lost about where to begin getting the information and help they need. Unlike Lutheran General Hospital, where Kathryn was born, with the help of doctors like Dr. Mangurten heading the NICU, too many other facilities are not equipped to help these families.

Parents of disabled children who attend public school special needs programs often experience different frustrations. After twelve years of school and graduation, their special needs children may end up with the dilemma of what's next. School systems need counselors who are willing and able to help transition these children into the real world, but not all schools offer this type of service. Some would qualify for a job program, but it is necessary to have a professional to guide them along this path. Parents help if they are aggressive, but too often, they are at a complete loss as to where they should begin. These people will have a tough adjustment if they don't get the guidance they need. A support group is a good place to start.

Trials are meant to bring us closer to God, to take our eyes off of the here and now, and put our focus on eternity. God doesn't want any to perish, so to accomplish this He does whatever it takes to turn us back to Him. The Bible says that trials are like refining gold. In order for gold to be valuable, it has to go through the fire. Without the refining, gold is just a piece of rock.

6) Planning ahead gives you peace of mind.

What will happen to their disabled child is a concern for parents as they reach certain milestones. Many of these children will outlive their parents. While it is natural for children to live longer than their parents do, it poses a problem for special needs people. "What will happen when we die?" parents ask. "What is going to happen to my child if we get sick and can't take care of them?" Waiting lists at good homes that would take over the responsibilities of these parents when they get too old or die range anywhere from five to twenty years. That in itself is a frightening prospect for aging parents.

Parents of disabled children need a good attorney to help

make provisions for the care of the child. An attorney specializing in wills and trusts specifically for disabled people can help parents get their concerns answered and affairs for their child settled. Parents should not put off making these arrangements.

My friend, Kay, taught me a valuable lesson about leaving the bulk of these details to God. As her guardian and the executor of her estate, I was concerned about her well-being when she was in her late eighties living across the country from me. I said, "I'm really worried about you. What's going to happen to you if you get sick and can't take care of yourself?"

She answered, "Barbie, God has taken care of me for eighty-seven years. He's not going to stop now."

Even with that kind of trust in God, we talked about what she would like to see happen if she couldn't manage by herself at home. Kay had a plan already set that made it easier for her to continue to be independent in her home in California until she died. Kay's life and plans should be an example. She looked at her options and decided on a course of action before her situation was beyond her control. Parents need to have such a course of action for their children who cannot make plans for themselves.

For the disabled, planning for education, what to do after formal schooling has been completed, concerns for living after parental caregivers are gone, and legal concerns are real challenges. It can be helpful when churches get involved with disability ministries, offering resources and programs to assist in such decisions. Partnering with help agencies such as Joni and Friends or other social agencies can also ease the burden. Compassionate, supportive people can accomplish much when they become involved in helping parents get help for their child.

After I retired, it became my desire to be an advocate for the disabled. Seeing the importance of these documents, I realize parents of disabled people need encouragement and guidance to get these legal papers in order. This has now become the biggest part of the H.I.M. Ministry.

Cheryl Noll is a friend from church with three daughters. Two out of the three have special needs. In 2006, Cheryl phoned me to ask if I would help her arrange guardianship for Katie, her oldest daughter, who had just turned eighteen years old. Though handicapped, she is extremely gregarious, happy, and social.

Agreeing to help Cheryl and Katie, the three of us took the train downtown to the courthouse. Katie talked to everyone. Several times Cheryl said, "Don't talk to strangers. Put on your headphones and listen to your music." We got off the train and walked up the stairs to the street level. Immediately, Katie turned to the girl walking beside her and asked, "What's your name?" The girl said, "Lisa." Cheryl reprimanded Katie and said, "I told you not to talk to strangers." Katie answered, "She's not a stranger. I know her. Her name is Lisa." Her comment cracked us up.

Eventually the court date arrived, and Cheryl asked me if I would go to the hearing with her, her husband, Art, and Katie. When we got to court, the clerk saw how "social" Katie was. He told Cheryl he would fit her in early, so Katie's socialization would not disturb court proceedings. The Nolls were called, and Art, Cheryl, and Katie stood in front of the judge. Katie turned around several times, motioning me to join them. The judge noticed and asked Katie who I was. She replied, "She's my friend." The judge asked me my name, and said, "Barbara, please come up and stand next to your friend."

Cheryl and her family first came to our church when they learned of the H.I.M. disability ministry. She and I now run the ministry together. One of the goals of H.I.M. is to integrate and include the disabled in ministry and activities performed by healthy teenagers. Rich and I have called on Cheryl's other special needs daughter, Patti, to babysit for us. Usually, Kathryn is in bed when she comes, and Patti is capable of calling her mother if an emergency should arise. She feels good about her ability to help, especially when she goes home with her very own paycheck.

Discussions between spouses and guardians regarding custody and care are necessary for all concerned before making decisions. These legal steps need to be taken no matter how overwhelming. As parents of disabled children, since our children cannot make decisions, we need to make the best plans we can for their future. After we've done our best, God will do the rest. He loves our children more than we do.

7) Everybody handles trials differently.

Erma Bombeck wrote an article responding to feedback and reactions from her readers about, "The Valiant Mother." When my sister sent me the reply to this Bombeck article, I realized that not everyone with a disabled child shared my positive opinions and feelings of gratitude. Some have not come to grips with the responsibility of a child who will always be a child. I needed to deal with my naïveté as I read Bombeck's article about the reactions of some readers.

Erma Bombeck said she has never in sixteen years received such an overwhelming response to an article she had published. The responses ranged from people who didn't want to talk about the grossly retarded and resented the attention Bombeck gave them in her article to a couple letters that doubted that such children even came from God as He only makes perfect children.

There was also legitimate criticism from social workers and

organizations working with these families that they should not be patronized. They stated that these families have a hard enough time just coping and should not have to feel guilty. Many gained strength through having a disabled child; others drowned in their inability to cope.

Yet another letter said that parents in general lack patience with their children, handicapped or not. They felt the focus on the disabled was unnecessary.

Another woman wrote that she had a severely retarded, hyperactive child, and they as her parents decided to place her in an institution. She was less than God intended, and her new living situation allowed them to get on with their lives. They were concerned that Bombeck's article made their decision more difficult, and they shouldn't be made to feel guilty. They said, "There is no single answer, and we need not try to be saints."

Ninety-five percent of the letters were from mothers of disabled children who knew they were not saints but said the article was encouraging.

One woman said she had two handicapped children, and she loved them, not because they were handicapped, but because they were her children.

Parents with normal children rarely experience what one mother did. Her handicapped child had played day after day with only a bucket for five years. One day he asked for a toy for Christmas. The mother cried for three hours and then bought out the toy store.

Another comment was that BJ was her mid-life crisis baby. She said, "I don't see a saint when I look in the mirror, but I'm a better person because of him."

One daughter, who was born with multiple handicaps, died

millimeter by millimeter. The mother ranted and raved at God a thousand times and told Him He was scum. She wondered why God gave His son only three hours of suffering before death, while her child was going through years of torment. After five years, she finally accepted her situation, knowing it was where she needed to be at that time in her life.

Some mothers of handicapped children felt they were dealt a bad hand of cards, yet, each one plays her hand in her own way. Some have a tougher time than others do buying the Biblical admonition that God never gives you more than you can handle. Some begged for understanding and wisdom. One mother said that a little humor could save a life—her own.

Bombeck received photos, cards, and personal stories from all over the world. Some requested that fathers and siblings be given credit since they also lived with the problem, but most of the notes said that her column made them feel good, and they needed that.

This column showed the readers the emotional turmoil and hurt some families feel when ignorance, cruelty, and prejudice are directed at disabled children and their families.

Bombeck ended the column with a version of the poem "Footprints," written in 1936 by Mary Stevenson.

Footprints in the Sand

One night I dreamed I was walking along
the beach with the Lord.
Many scenes from my life flashed across the sky.
In each scene I noticed footprints in the sand.
Sometimes there were two sets of footprints,
other times there was one only.

This bothered me because I noticed that
during the low periods of my life,
when I was suffering from anguish, sorrow or defeat,
I could see only one set of footprints, so I said to the Lord,

"You promised me Lord that if I followed you,
you would walk with me always.
But I have noticed that during the most trying periods
of my life there has only been one set of footprints in the sand.
Why, when I needed you most, have you not been there for me?"

The Lord replied, "The years when you have seen
only one set of footprints, my child,
is when I carried you."

Bombeck's article illustrates the five steps people often experience in dealing with grief. With the birth, illness, death, and disappointment of a disabled child, family members go through denial, anger, guilt, negotiation, and finally acceptance or resolution in successfully dealing with their grief. Some people get stuck at one stage or another and are unable to reach resolution. Rich and I have experienced all of these steps in coming to an acceptance of our family situation. The article shouldn't have come as a surprise to me, but it pointed out how naive we can be, especially me! Until something horrific happens in life, we sometimes think bad things only happen to other people. During pregnancy and into childhood, parents imagine how their child will turn out. When a disabled child is born or a disabling illness, accident, or tragedy happens, we grieve the loss of our dreams. All go through some form of grieving, but the process can be different for each person. Some go back and forth between anger and negotiation.

Some dwell on denial and anger for a long period of time. Other grievers might never get through the whole process, and that can cause problems like depression, uncontrolled anger, and, too often, divorce.

Some people go through the different stages in another order or backtrack and repeat stages. It is important that we grieve and end up at the acceptance or resolution phase. Sooner rather than later is best for each family member.

8) If you accept your child's disability, so will your friends.

Accepting a disabled person into the family, by birth, accident, or illness, is not only hard on the family, it is hard for relatives and friends also. One sad and difficult challenge for us is to hear some in our support group say that many of their close friends stop calling and visiting. We experienced this at Kathryn's birth. Fortunately, we immediately realized it was going to be up to us to make our friends feel comfortable around our daughter and us. Once we implemented our plan, our friends and family were accepting of our situation and Kathryn's disabilities.

Through the years, people asked how they should address Kathryn's problem. It seems that putting a label on Kathryn's condition is a stumbling block for some. "Should we say she's disabled, handicapped, retarded, and/or multi-handicapped? What term are you comfortable with?" they asked.

Our answer was and is always the same. It doesn't matter to us how people refer to Kathryn. Being politically correct isn't going to change her condition. So, whatever each person is comfortable with, that's fine with us. All we ask is that people love and respect Kathryn just the way she is.

Our friends and family are not afraid to use the "R" word (retarded). They speak freely about Kathryn's problems, and we are glad our good friends support and encourage us. Some of their level of comfort may be because we have accepted Kathryn's condition. As we allow others to see we have accepted her disabilities, they are also able to do so.

In the 80s, it was common for children to say, "Oh, yeah, you're retarded." One day, I was coming up the stairs to my aunt's house in Chicago and my cousin was outside playing with one of his friends. They must have had a disagreement about something as one of them said, "You're retarded." I stopped in my tracks and said, "Kathryn's retarded," and turned to walk into the house. Since both of them knew Kathryn, they must have given this some thought. I never heard them use the "R" word again.

Parents of special needs children sometimes experience depression. Curbing complaints about your problems and being able to see the positive, good aspects of your life, your child, and your family is hard to muster when you are in the midst of serious difficulties. Having a Pollyanna attitude of how wonderful life is does not lessen the burden of a tough situation. Maintaining a happy medium is more realistic, and people gravitate to those who are able to keep that balance.

Our friends remained supportive when they saw us coping in a realistic, appropriate way. Rich and I knew our friends grieved with us and felt our pain. True friends gave us space when we were involved in the many health issues we needed to address for Kathryn. We took it upon ourselves to reassure our friends and family that we would get through these difficulties as we had other problems before. This inclusion into our personal lives gives them a connection with the three of us that helps maintain our lifelong friendships.

Sometimes I've put up a courageous front on the outside to my friends and our family. I was not so brave all the time, however. I often awoke in the middle of the night crying. Rich would ask what bothered me, I would tell him, and he would hold and console me. He would tell me to get it all out, knowing that a part of grieving for me was expressing my pain through tears.

Kay Hager was a blessing for me during this time. Sometimes I needed to throw myself a pity-party, or complain about every little annoyance. Kay listened. She consoled me. She encouraged me. After our conversation was over, I didn't feel a need to share my problems with anyone else. One mature friend who supports you and listens to your concerns when your world seems to be crumbling is essential to making it through the maze of depression and grief. Choose that person carefully: a good listener, an encourager, not someone who allows you to wallow in your pain, pity you, or drag you further into depression.

9) Take it one day at a time.

"Why me, Lord?" That question was constantly on my mind the first days after Kathryn's birth, and I wasn't using it in a positive sense. I felt guilty about questioning God until I came to the conclusion that it's okay to honestly ask the Lord why things happen in life. Many mothers of special needs children cry out and question Him. When Kathryn was born, I certainly did. At one point, I felt God was punishing Kathryn for my sins. I asked why He would punish her for my wrongs. Until we ask and receive answers from God, we live with useless guilt.

It was a blessing when I finally realized that God is a God of love. What happened to my daughter helped me grow to be the person God intended. I feel at peace when I follow His instructions as in Matthew 6:33 & 34: *"But seek first His kingdom and His righteousness and all these things shall be added to you. Therefore do not be anxious for tomorrow; for tomorrow will take care of itself. Each day has enough trouble of its own."*

I developed a new set of mottos for myself: "Stay close to God," "Seek to do His will," "Don't worry about tomorrow," and "Take one day at a time."

Daily, moment by moment I reinforced this thinking by imprinting a Cristy Lane song, called "One Day at a Time," on my mind. The beginning of the song, which is with me to this day, goes like this:

One Day at a Time

Written by Marijohn Wilkin and Kris Kristofferson
Buckhorn Music Publishing, Incorporated
Nashville, Tennessee
Used with permission

I'm only human, I'm just a woman
Help me believe in what I can be and all that I am.
Show me the stairway I have to climb
Lord for my sake, teach me to take
One day at a time.

One day at a time, Sweet Jesus,
That's all I'm asking from you
Just give me the strength to do every day
What I have to do.

Yesterday's gone, Sweet Jesus,
And tomorrow may never be mine.
Lord help me today, show me the way
One day at a time.

When I first heard this song on the radio, I bought the CD. It constantly reminds me to take things one day at a time, to live in the present, and not to dwell in the past or project myself needlessly into an unknown, uncertain future. I have since bought several copies to give to parents of newborns with disabilities.

Patiently taking one day at a time was a hard concept for people like me who worried about everything. I remember talking to Rich about Kathryn's future. In his wisdom, he reassured me, reiterating the words of Cristy's song long before we ever heard it: "Honey, just take it one day at a time. Don't worry about that now."

I argued with him, "That's easy for you. You're busy at work everyday. I'm at home taking care of Kathryn, and the reality stares me in the face every minute of every day."

The worrying continued until one day I received an invitation to come and hear Dr. Kenneth Moses speak at Lutheran General Hospital. His talk was inspiring. As a counselor to parents of disabled children, he had been doing this work for years before he and his wife had a disabled child of their own. After his son was born, he understood and empathized with his clients. He spoke with experience and authority. His words were just right for me. After the meeting, I approached him and said, "I worry about my daughter all the time. I'm afraid of what's going to happen to her if something happens to my husband or me."

Dr. Moses' answer sent me home to tell Rich about his talk. "I wish you'd gone with me to hear Dr. Moses! He was fabulous!

He put into words everything I've been feeling. He knows what we're going through. After the meeting, I went up to him and told him how I worry about Kathryn's future. He made me feel calm and secure. I will never worry about her again." My words spilled out as Rich listened.

"Really? What did he say?" Rich asked, smiling.

"He told me not to worry. He said to take things one day at a time. I'm not supposed to be so uptight." Again, one word spilled out on top of the other.

Rich's face broke out into a grin. "Sounds familiar! I've been telling you that for years. Why did you believe him and not me?'

"Maybe it was the letters after his name," I joked.

It wasn't that the doctor had a magic bullet. Nor was it because he had a Ph.D. or that he was more educated than many people. Rich really had been giving me this same good advice for several years. Until that evening, I wasn't ready to accept it. That night, though, my mind and spirit were ready to hear and process his good advice.

The key to dealing with any adversity is getting through it one day at a time and not worrying about a future that may never happen. In all of life's challenges, large or small, God is there if we're ready to trust Him...one day at a time.

10) Anger should be short-lived.

Occasionally, I have been asked if I ever get angry at God...or someone else. Being honest, I answer that question, "You bet I do!" It certainly didn't seem God was such a fair judge or careful protector when the day my child was born I was told she wasn't going to live, and that same evening a mother tried to drown her perfectly healthy baby. I was never angrier with God than that day. I lay in a hospital bed praying for my child to live, and another woman was trying to kill hers. How could a loving, compassionate, just God allow that?

After Kathryn was born and was almost a year old, Rich and I became referral parents to others with handicapped children. Donna was one of these parents. Her son, Ricky, had the same condition Kathryn had, microcephaly. He also was a dwarf. His brain damage was in a different location from Kathryn's, so while Kathryn was blind, Ricky could see, and he could walk. He also had major hearing loss. The two children had different problems, but with Ricky's typical microcephaly facial features, when I looked at him, his cute face appealed to me. He reminded me of my little girl, and I immediately cared about what happened to him and his family.

Donna called me one day, crying. Taking Ricky out in public was becoming more than she could bear. People starred at Ricky, and Donna was sensitive to the attention they were getting. After much convincing, she agreed to try once more to ignore the stares and make a trip to the grocery store that same day. A few hours later Donna called again. This time she was hysterical. I finally pieced together what occurred at the grocery store.

While Donna pushed her cart with little Ricky in his infant seat, she crossed paths with a woman who said, "Is that a dog you have in the grocery cart?" To this day, I find Donna and Ricky's story unbelievable. What reasonable, humane person would ever say such a thing? It took almost an hour to calm Donna down and reassure her that the woman was not the norm. Donna just happened to run into an unusually tactless person. This insensitivity is devastating to any parent or sibling of a handicapped child.

Donna and her husband were great parents for any child,

handicapped or not. Donna became less sensitive about people's rude remarks and became Ricky's biggest advocate. As Ricky grew, so did their love for him. His parents were devastated when they found out that their son was going to need a kidney transplant. Their concern was even greater when they were told that there were only so many kidneys to go around. Because of Ricky's severe handicaps, he wouldn't be considered for one of the available organs. Donna's husband decided to be his son's donor; he would give Ricky one of his kidneys. Sadly, Ricky died at age ten, shortly after the transplant.

Another time that I got upset was after Kathryn's brain surgery. When the worst was over, I decided it was time for me to go back to work part-time. Since my former position in personnel was no longer available, I took a position working for the Advertising Manager at Dynascan. Larry, my boss, was older, probably well into his sixties. He had a married daughter, and he and his wife lived alone in their large suburban home. I knew Larry before I took maternity leave, but I was still surprised at what happened the first day on the job. Larry heard about Kathryn before I came to work for him, and he asked how Kathryn was doing. I told him we were doing well, pleased that he was concerned enough to ask.

His next words did not please me. "It's too bad your daughter lived!"

Disbelievingly I said, "Too bad for who, Larry? I'm glad she's still alive and with us."

Knowing Larry from my previous years working at the company, I understood a bit of how he thought and where his priorities lay. The worst thing that ever happened to him was when someone threw stones on his driveway. Larry hired a private detective to find out who was pranking them, and prosecuted the childish culprits when they were caught. In the couple of years I worked for Larry, I constantly had to remind myself that his priorities were different from mine.

The majority of people we've encountered when we're out with Kathryn accompanying us are kind and considerate. There were only a couple incidents I would rather forget.

It was about a week before Christmas in 1990 when our friends, Georgette and Dennis, wanted us to go out to dinner with them, and later we were to exchange gifts at their home. We normally would get a babysitter to stay with Kathryn, but because of the busy season, none were available. We decided to take her with us to a nice restaurant in Chicago.

When we got to the restaurant, the hostess seated us in one of the smaller dining rooms. Just outside this room, we could hear other small children running around and making noise. Kathryn was hungry. She often lets us know she wants to eat with loud sounds, and she did this as usual. The people in our dining area didn't seem to be disturbed by her, but the manager/ owner of the restaurant was. He came to our table and knelt down next to me. "Is she going to continue making those loud sounds all evening? She is disturbing the other people in this dining room," he said.

"She's just hungry. When she gets something to eat she will be quiet," I reassured him.

"I certainly hope so," he answered rather curtly.

My husband and I were so humiliated and embarrassed we decided we should leave. Our friends agreed. As we got up, several of the other customers noticed.

"You don't have to leave. She isn't bothering us at all," one of the diners said.

We thanked them, and said we didn't feel comfortable staying.

The waitress working that dining room also made a comment. "Please don't leave. Your little girl isn't bothering anyone."

That was the first and only time we took Kathryn out because someone said something offensive to us. I decided to write a letter to the owner of the restaurant hoping that his apology would soothe our angry feelings and give closure to an unpleasant experience. In the letter, I wrote that it was by the grace of God that no one in his immediate family was born with a disability. I told him that he should thank God for his good health. Although an apology never came, a few years later we heard on a sports radio channel that this restaurant was running a contest that would benefit an organization helping disabled people. We hoped the letter had some impact on the owner. It showed me that you never know how your influence will change a heart or improve a negative situation.

Around midnight twenty-three days after Kathryn's third birthday, I got a call from my sister. Rich answered the telephone since he often got calls from work in the middle of the night. I heard Richard's side of the conversation and knew that it was my sister Pat who was calling. "Oh, no, Pat, what happened?" It didn't sound good. At the time, my father was ill with emphysema, so I would naturally have made the assumption that something happened to Dad. Instead, I immediately had the strong feeling that my older brother, only thirty-eight years old at the time, was dead, and that he committed suicide. I have no idea why I would have thought this, but that was exactly what had happened. Eddie took a syringe filled with the drug they use to put animals to sleep at the lab where he worked. He was dead… by his own hand. I was devastated and confused. Why would my wonderful older brother do such a thing? Why would a successful man take his own life?

Eddie was a self-made man. He had put himself through college, then got masters and doctoral degrees in biology, and did some post graduate work. He struggled his first year of college and barely passed, but he was determined to succeed. He was mild mannered, polite, funny, good looking, successful, and had a beautiful wife. His home was lovely, and he was well liked by everyone. I thought these were all the things that society says are so important. I couldn't imagine why he killed himself.

The morning after I learned of my brother's death, I went into the small hallway of our house between the bedrooms and screamed at the top of my lungs, "God, why are you doing all these terrible things? If this is all I'll ever have in my life, then I just want to die, too. But, if there is a reason, then show me because I can't make any sense out of my life right now."

Five years later, I began to see what God was trying to show me, and my life did indeed begin to make sense.

My brother Eddie was a devout Catholic in high school. He wanted to become a priest. In college, he majored in science. As he studied in secular universities, he began to believe more and more in evolution and less and less in God. Eventually, he became an atheist. As my brother fell away from his faith, I realized how important my faith in God was.

Eddie's wife told him she wanted a divorce. In his mind, this was the first and only failure of his life. Eddie probably felt he had nowhere to turn. Dad was sick, and my Mom had to take care of him, so Eddie didn't want to bother them with his problems. My sister was still dealing with her own demons. My younger brother was also having problems.

Ed rarely called me; sometimes as much as four years went by without a phone call, letter, or card from him. Just before he killed himself, for the first time in years, he called me four times in one month. Each time he would ask for an update on Kathryn, and my news was always disturbing. She was scheduled for her third surgery. There was a possibility of a fourth operation in six months. She was recovering from one of the surgeries. My brother certainly didn't feel he could share his problems when I was dealing with my own serious troubles. He never confided in any of us in the family. I've assumed his loneliness and despair must have made him decide to commit suicide.

For several years, I felt guilty and agonized that I didn't help my brother when he obviously was reaching out to me with those phone calls. Eventually I came to terms with this guilt, realizing that although he called for help, he never told me that he was desperate and depressed. I still wonder if he would be alive today had he been honest about his suicidal feelings.

Anger is like a canker sore. Left untreated it can fester and infect your spirit and other parts of your body. Like a raging river, unresolved anger can flood into other areas of your life. It is like a bubbling stew that will brew inside until you explode. I experienced this kind of anger when my brother Eddie took his life.

My parents, sister, Aunt Bernice, and I went to the funeral in Texas. Eddie's father-in-law met my aunt and me at the airport, and we waited an hour for my family to arrive from Arizona. I was in shock that my wonderful brother was gone. My sister and parents walked off the plane, and we hurried over to greet them.

Mom's eyes looked sad and questioning. My dad however had a specific agenda on his mind. Before meeting or greeting anyone, he asked, "Could we have one of Eddie's automobiles for my son Jimmy? Helen won't need two cars and my younger son really could use one." Those were the first words out of his mouth! Not, "How did it happen? Is Helen okay? Can we see Eddie now?" We were all embarrassed. I was furious at Dad's insensitivity.

Our family's dysfunction was more aptly illustrated again the next morning when we went out for breakfast before going to the undertaker. During breakfast, my sister said something to my mother that made her angry. My mother turned, looked at the both of us, and said, "I wish God had taken the two of you and left me Eddie."

To my sister, my younger brother, and me, it was no secret that Eddie was Mom's favorite child. Her three other children had known of her blatant favoritism for years. Our mother's uncaring, hurtful words to us at a time when our family needed to be united devastated me then and for years after.

It soon became obvious that my parents blamed Helen for Eddie's death. When we got to Eddie's house, Dad made comments blaming Helen. I was appalled and reassured Helen that no one was responsible for Eddie's death except Eddie himself. My parents blamed Helen because she wanted a divorce; they figured if she hadn't asked for the divorce, he wouldn't have committed suicide. Helen didn't kill Eddie. Eddie chose to put the needle in his arm knowing it would kill him. It wasn't my sister-in-law's fault, my parents weren't to blame, nor was it God's fault. From my parent's viewpoint, though, someone had to be responsible. It was plain and simple; Eddie made the last and worst choice of his life.

Up until his marriage failed, Eddie had experienced no major failures. He had been good at everything he did. Truly, he did love Helen and was devastated when she wanted to end their marriage. However, he was the one who put the lethal injection into his veins; no one made him do it.

God gave me a peace in the midst of the turmoil of that horrible time. I was able to ignore the unkind words expressed those three days in Texas. I was facing Kathryn's second surgery upon my arrival home from Eddie's funeral and I didn't have the time, energy, or will to deal with them at that time. I hid them in my subconscious mind for many years until I was stronger and more capable of dealing with the years of pent up emotions and hurts.

My younger brother Jimmy lived in the shadow of my older brother all his life. We weren't very close after he moved to Arizona with my parents and I got involved with Lennie. After Kathryn was born, our relationship drifted even further because she needed a lot of my personal attention, and traveling was not much of an option for me.

Living with our parents was hard for Jimmy. Even though my father quit drinking once they moved to Arizona, his controlling personality made him a difficult person to live with. After Jimmy graduated from Scottsdale Community College, he joined the Air Force on August 20, 1974. Three years later, he met and married his first wife, Linda.

They remained married, though Linda had an affair and left him for several months. When she returned, she was pregnant, and her daughter, Amanda, was born in November of 1978 with hydrocephaly. A tube drained the fluid in her head, and Amanda seemed to be doing well. If the surgery is done in a timely fashion, usually these children grow up without further complications. Jimmy accepted this child as his own, and gave her his name, but Linda left him shortly after Amanda's birth. They divorced in 1982. He never saw Linda or Amanda again.

In 1985, Jimmy met Ingrid and they were engaged. Rich, Kathryn, and I were pleased to attend the wedding in Arizona. I prayed that this time he would have a wonderful marriage and life, but that didn't happen. Jimmy lost his job and had a hard time finding another one. My parents supplemented by helping out with his bills. The financial stress and pressure pushed Ingrid to file for a divorce in 1990, the same year my father died.

Jimmy moved in with my mother to cut his expenses and give my mother a companion in the house. This turned out to be a good move for both of them. As my mother got older and started forgetting to take her medicine, Jimmy was there to help.

In 1999, my younger brother had a bicycle accident that changed his life forever. Being in a wheelchair for several months caused him to put on weight. He began to have difficulties breathing. Having been in the Air Force, he qualified for services from the Veteran's Hospital in Phoenix and was diagnosed with congestive heart failure and COPD (Chronic Obstructive Pulmonary Disease), a serious lung disease that, over time, makes it hard to breathe. Upon investigating his situation, it was determined that the Air Force should never have accepted him because he had asthma, and that his experiences while in the Air Force, with close interaction with chemicals being tested for chemical warfare, had caused greater damage to his lungs, causing the COPD and congestive heart failure. He was put on permanent disability.

Though he's had some hard knocks, Jimmy is a smart, caring, and generous person. When his disability checks came in, he used part of the money to help my mother. He replaced major appliances in her house and treated her with dignity and respect. She began to appreciate her younger son giving praise and consideration which helped him to start feeling better about himself. His low self esteem from early on and feeling second best to my brother Eddie took a toll on his personality. Recently, he's felt more optimistic and feels he's been given a second chance at life.

In February of 2003, Jimmy's kidneys failed, and he wasn't expected to live. However, he made an amazing recovery and was able to come home after a month in a Scottsdale rehabilitation center. By that time, my mother could not be left by herself. She didn't want to come to Chicago to live with me. My sister was going through another episode of her illness and couldn't take care of her. By God's amazing grace, I got her into an assisted living situation in one day's time. The social worker helping me said that she had never been able to get anyone into a facility in less than two weeks. We prayed and God answered. Jimmy came home and seemed to be doing better for a while. In 2007, he was diagnosed with MRSA, a serious staph infection, and nearly died. He again miraculously recovered, however, this weakened his lungs, and now he uses oxygen all the time.

Jimmy's life is a miracle. Twice he wasn't supposed to live, and twice he survived. He told me that he felt God kept him alive for a reason.

I agreed and said, "Jimmy, God's kept you alive so that you could ask Jesus into your heart."

He shrugged his shoulders and said, "Maybe?"

Most of my life, I've had more anger toward my mother than my alcoholic father. He was drunk; my mother wasn't. I questioned why she didn't stand up to him and stick up for us. I wondered why she allowed my dad to physically abuse my sister and older brother. I imagined what life would have been if she had left him and raised us peacefully.

Where anger reigns, God has His work cut out for Him. He melted my heart. In October of 1996, after my mission's trip with Joni and Friends to deliver wheelchairs to Poland, I stayed another week visiting relatives and visiting the farm in Poland where my mother was raised. Seeing how and where she grew up helped me understand her better. The primitive conditions and backward lifestyle that some of our older Polish relatives still live under were foreign to me. Though my relatives in Poland were happy and content, I could see why my mother was so intent on making her marriage and her life in America work out. Mom never had a formal education. With no schooling, she couldn't earn enough money to raise us by herself. She didn't drive a car. There was no escape for her. She had a life with my father that was far above what she could have had in Europe, and she knew it.

As I analyzed my feelings, I realized that a lot of my anger was because my mother didn't show an interest in my life, before or after I had Kathryn. She never called me. She never asked about Kathryn. She never asked me how I was doing. I wanted her to ask, "Is it hard to care for your daughter?" I longed to hear her say, "I love you." I felt as if Kathryn and I didn't exist in my mother's life. One year when I called my mother, she was complaining about how hot it was in Arizona. I offered to buy her an airplane ticket so she could come to Chicago and spend a month or two with us until the weather cooled down in Arizona. Her answer hurt my feelings, "All my friends in Chicago are dead. There's nothing left for me in Chicago anymore." What were Richard, Kathryn, and I...chopped chicken liver? Incidents like this further confirmed the doubts I had about my mother's love.

My mother was an unhappy woman. Whenever we did speak, her conversations focused on the past. Even years after she left Poland and my father died, she still brought up what had gone before, especially details about how hard life was. She rarely had anything positive to say. She lived her entire life in yesterday. All this anger and bitterness played havoc with her health. She battled cancer three times. When I was fourteen years old, she had surgery for uterine cancer. In her early seventies she had a mastectomy. She died of lung cancer on November 25, 2006, never knowing the joy and happiness of today.

Eventually my anger against Mom turned to empathy. I

read my Bible, and I knew God was asking me to forgive her. Gradually, I gave up my hard heart and hurt feelings, let go of my anger, and accepted my mother unconditionally. I focused on her good points. She had taken good care of us growing up. She often made our clothes. She was a good cook, kept a neat house, and made sure that we had clean clothes for school. God showed me that, with her own emotional needs so unfulfilled, Mom never learned how to meet the emotional needs of others.

I confided in my friend Fergus that I had finally forgiven my mother. He told me several months earlier I needed to forgive if I was to get on with my own life. I thought he was going to be overjoyed; I expected he might even pin the proverbial medal on my chest. I was puzzled when I saw the expression on his face. It wasn't happiness. He read me exactly right knowing I expected a pat on the back. I asked, "Fergus, aren't you happy that I was able to forgive my mother?"

He nodded and said, "Sure I am."

I heard a "but" in his voice, so I asked, "But, what? What's wrong?"

Fergus hesitated. "I'm not sure you want to hear this, Barb." His voice gave me fair warning that he was right.

Fergus and I had developed a level of trust, so I wanted to hear what he had to say. I pressed him. "Yes, I do. What's wrong?"

Fergus looked me in the eye and asked, "Have you asked your mother to forgive you?"

I was speechless! I couldn't imagine what I, a most devoted, dutiful, caring daughter, needed to be forgiven for. There was never a question in my mind that I hadn't been a good daughter. Our talk ended there, however, and we parted ways.

That night I couldn't sleep. Though Fergus and I were good friends, I was angry. As I tossed and turned, the Lord did some talking. I listened to His still, small voice speaking through my conscience. God whispered that I did need my mother's forgiveness, and my mother needed to give it. My mother was uneducated and quite helpless in so many ways. I realized she didn't call me because the whole telephone "thing" was intimidating to her. I should have taught her how to dial the phone. I also hadn't taken the time and effort to teach her how to drive. Question after question followed by answer after answer popped into my head. The Lord was bombarding me with another side of my own story. He was showing me what I needed to do.

It took a week to muster up the courage to call her. We chatted for almost a half of an hour before I said what was on my mind. I knew I needed to ask for her forgiveness before she decided it was time to hang up.

I blurted it out. "Mom, I called to ask you to forgive me for not being a good daughter."

Mom used my Polish nickname. "Bas, what are you talking about? You've been a very good daughter to me." She continued saying I'd never given her a bit of trouble, she'd never had to worry about me because I was doing so well on my own. She said I was a great housekeeper, a good wife to Richard, and she wished her marriage had been as good as Rich's and mine. She was glad that we had such a good life together. She also said something I had wanted to hear for years. My mother told me she admired the way I was taking care of Kathryn and how hard it must be. Then I heard the words I desired to hear more than any other! She said, "I love you very much, Bas." In forty minutes, she had said everything I had been waiting forty-five years to hear. I was overjoyed, and it felt as if a heavy weight was lifted from deep down.

In the next few months, I thought about the words I'd longed to hear for my whole life. Though it was good to hear Mom say them and know finally that my mother did love me, her words didn't change my life in any way. I was the same before our conversation as afterward. I wracked my brain to think why my mother's approval was so important to me. After all, I had Rich's approval, and, more importantly, I had God's approval. Why did I feel I must hear Mom confess her love and concern for me? I realized this was how the devil was able to gain a foothold in my life. As long as my focus was on the anger issue, it hindered any opportunities to do constructive work for God. Many people, even "good Christians," fall into this trap of Satan.

After that forgiveness phone conversation, my mother never ended another of our long distance chats without telling me she loved me. Our whole relationship changed. Fergus was right. Forgiveness is a two-way street, and I needed to travel it.

11) Take control of your child's medical needs.

People place a lot of faith in the experience, knowledge, and competence of their doctors. Parents of disabled children are no exception to this; they are probably more guilty than most. Dr. Mangurten once told us that we knew Kathryn better than he did as she was in our constant care. He felt that in some instances this qualified us more than him to make some judgment calls about her health issues.

Kathryn had her first minor seizure while she was still in the NICU at Lutheran General Hospital. After the seizure, the doctor prescribed Phenobarbital for her. She was on this medication for three years. The meds made her tired and lethargic all the time. As she got older, she began pushing the spoon away, making me spill out more than she ingested. I tasted it, and it was awful. I told Rich how bad it tasted.

"If she isn't going to live much longer, why should we keep making her take this awful stuff?"

He agreed, and we decided to quit force-feeding her medicine.

At Kathryn's six-month check up, Doctor Mangurten was impressed with her progress. "She looks great. She is more active and alert than your last visit."

"We do keep her busy. She goes swimming in the pool with water wings. She loves the independence this allows her. She is also doing patty cake." I showed him pictures of Kathryn in our friend's pool. You could see the look of independence on her face.

He was pleased to see such great improvement. Then came the dreaded question. "How much Phenobarbital are you giving her now?"

Sheepishly, but truthfully, I answered, "None."

Dr. Mangurten smiled. "That's great. No wonder she is so much more alert and active."

I looked at him curiously. "If that's so great then why didn't you take her off the meds?"

"I couldn't," he reluctantly replied.

Doctors are being sued so frequently now that they some-times take precautions to avoid such actions. Please note: *I am certainly not advising anyone to take their child off of medications prescribed by their doctor.* However, sometimes we need to wisely research and question what is being done for our child. The health and well-being of our children is ultimately our responsibility as parents.

12) Maintain a good sense of humor.

Rich and I have been blessed with a strong, happy marriage. I praise God and give Him all the credit for our successful third of a century together. During the difficult times when Kathryn was young and going through many medical procedures, Rich was my strength. As well as being a deeply caring person, he stays strong and keeps his good sense of humor. If he thinks I am worried, he will take my mind off the problem by injecting a funny comment. One time he said to me, "When you get mad at me, I'm going to kiss you. Who can stay mad at a person who is kissing them?" His sense of humor and compassion has helped our marriage endure.

When Rich turned fifty years old, I threw a surprise party for him. Many people got up to "roast" him. The roast lasted almost two hours, and people laughed hearing one story after another of Rich's "funny episodes." After the roast, my cousin Chris said to me, "That was so funny. How did people think up all those stories about Rich?" I told Chris, "They didn't make them up. Everything they said was true."

In his book, *Laugh Again*, Charles Swindoll writes, *"...joy is a choice. It is a matter of attitude that stems from one's confidence in God—that He is in full control, that He is in the midst of whatever has happened, is happening, and will happen. Either we fix our minds on that and determine to laugh again, or we wail and whine our way through life, complaining that we never got a fair shake. We are the ones who consciously determine which way we shall go."*

Little did I know when I married Richard what an encouragement he would be in my life. He has the ability to view things through clear eyes, with few prejudices or preconceptions. He helps us keep our lives balanced and sane. Richard also casts humor on many things that happen in our lives with Kathryn in a way that I cannot always do. He is my comic relief in a life story that sometimes becomes overwhelming.

It's hard to get mad at Richard when he makes a mistake, then laughs at himself, and doesn't get angry and frazzled. Laughter is a great tension breaker. Marriages are strengthened when couples maintain that good sense of humor through times of difficulty.

13) Disability isn't anyone's fault…It's God's plan to achieve His purpose for your life.

As strong as some marriages are, even the strongest sometimes crumble under heavy weight. Giving birth to and raising a disabled child is one of those heavy burdens. When husbands and wives are united, and the husband is supportive of his wife as she does most of the childcare for the disabled child, their marriage can survive. This is why I have said that it is important while going through these trials that you and your spouse maintain a good sense of humor or you will crumble under the weight of all the problems.

After the birth of a disabled child, I heard that the husband of one woman implied that it was her fault their child was born disabled. He told her after the delivery, "YOU have a disabled child." After the angry words were spoken, discussion and forgiveness were not shared and, sadly, that marriage ended in divorce. The disabled son suffered as his mother constantly pushed him to look and act "normal and healthy." No one benefited under the circumstances; the young boy suffered most of all.

I thank God that Rich and I had the wisdom not to play the blame game. Blame is destructive and doesn't change anything.

Accepting God's will for this child's life and watching God transform your life because of your willingness to trust and obey Him
is more productive. Although Rich never blamed me for Kathryn's
disability, another family member tried to. Rich's response was a
turning point in our marriage.

Grandparents are part of the family, especially in families
with disabled children. They are often a Godsend to shocked,
weary parents. When Kathryn came home from the hospital,
Rich's dad wanted us to bring her over so he could see her. When
we arrived at their home, Dad Blasco reached for her and held her
lovingly all evening. Looking at this new little granddaughter, he
couldn't understand what was so drastically wrong with her that
she wouldn't live.

Unlike his dad, Rich's mother didn't come into the living
room to see Kathryn the whole evening, and I became alarmed,
annoyed, and finally a bit angry. As it got late, we prepared to
leave, and I asked Ma if she wanted to see the baby. She finally
came into the living room and asked to hold Kathryn. She said
that Kathryn had Rich's chin and Rich's nose, but she had Polish
eyes.

I was furious! The encephalocele on the top of her head pulled
her forehead back, which made her eyes look funny. I concluded
that my mother-in-law was saying that I, the Polish wife, was
responsible for Kathryn's disability. I pulled Kathryn out of Ma's
arms and said loudly, "What the h... are Polish eyes?"

I stormed out of the house, and for the whole twenty-five
minute drive home, I used every curse word I'd ever heard, aimed
straight at my mother-in-law. I considered the conversation and
saw her comments as insults to me. Finally, I turned to Rich and
asked, "Aren't you going to say anything?"

The way I felt, no matter what Richard said, I would have

been furious. I was angry that he hadn't defended me, but God in His great wisdom gave him the words I needed to hear that day. He said kindly, in his usual gentle way, "Honey, she is my mother. She has always been this way. She will probably never change, but if you want we will never see her again."

Nothing else Richard could have said would have quenched my anger like those words. It was one of those "GOD MOMENTS" when the Lord speaks through a human, in this case, my husband. It put an instant end to my tirade.

It is usually the mother who deals with the disabled child day in and day out, and there is no escaping the many needs. Under the stress of caring for her disabled child, a woman's emotions are sometimes raw. She could drown in a sea of details and responsibilities if her husband does not support her.

Wives have to support their husbands also. From what I've seen, men don't go through the grieving process as quickly as women do. They often get caught and stuck in the denial stage.

After their child is born, the father can get back into a work routine, and earning a paycheck occupies their minds. Some men don't always deal with their deep emotions and concerns about this new life.

Communication is one of the most important ingredients in a marriage, but even more so when the marriage has to deal with a disabled child. It has been one of the strong points in our marriage, and Rich and I connect well verbally. He knew I would never keep him from his family, particularly his mother. After his supportive comments that day, I could handle any comment from my mother-in-law. Her piercing words no longer stung because I knew Rich supported me and knew how caustic his mother could be. Her insults came periodically, but I no longer took them personally. She treated everyone to stinging unkindness and sarcasm.

God also reminded me how I was never able to interact with special needs people before Kathryn was born. Possibly Ma Blasco also had this problem and her hands-off, untouchable reaction was her way of coping with our new challenges.

It's interesting that the first thing people notice and comment about are Kathryn's beautiful blue eyes. Sometimes I secretly say to myself, "Yes, they're Polish eyes." God has a sense of humor and His own unique way of healing our wounds.

14) Confront those who hurt you.

When I became a born again Christian, I read in the Bible that if someone says or does something hurtful to you, you need to confront them. What great advice. This is the quickest way to resolve a situation and keep you from hours, days, or months of useless anger and loss of peace. The next time my mother-in-law hurt my feelings I looked her right in the eye, and in a calm, quiet voice I asked, "Why would you say something like that to me? It's hurtful. If I said that to you, you would be devastated. Why do you think you can say something like that to me and not hurt my feelings?"

Ma Blasco was speechless. After that confrontation, she must have thought twice before speaking. The incidents of sharp words from my mother-in-law were fewer and farther between.

In 1998, Richard's mother fell and broke her wrist. She asked if she could come and stay with us until her wrist healed. I told her that we would always be there for her and I meant it! I was her caregiver for almost a month. We became fast friends, and though she never did interact with Kathryn much, her kindnesses toward me were encouraging. By opening our home and hearts, we showed her we cared. It was a life-changing experience for her.

She felt appreciated and loved, her anger dissolved, and in the last years of her life, she displayed a softer spirit.

Two weeks before Ma died, she had an aneurism in her brain and fell in the bathroom. The doctors said there would be some brain damage, but surgery would save her life. She refused the surgery three times. Hospice at the hospital was suggested. I refused hospital hospice; we would take care of her again in our home. She lived a week in a coma before she died. God gave me two opportunities to minister to my mother-in-law, and for that, I am grateful. Through it all, God gave me healing of anger, resentment, and hurt. Looking back on my relationship with my mother-in-law, I reflect on good times.

Focusing on problems and negativity is not profitable, especially when a caregiver needs to give one hundred percent of their energy to a disabled person. I've learned to practice the words of Scripture in Isaiah 58:10–11 *"Feed the hungry! Help those in trouble! Then your light will shine out from the darkness, and the darkness around will be bright as day. And the Lord will guide you continually, and satisfy you with all good things and keep you healthy too; and you will be like a well-watered garden, like an ever-flowing spring."* This reminds me to take my eyes off of my problems by using my energy to focus on the needs of others. When Kathryn's needs overwhelm me, I often go out and help someone. These words from Isaiah prove to be the best medicine in the world for Christians struggling with life's difficulties.

When I lose track of that focus, fortunately I have a husband who helps me regain the balance to be able to concentrate on positives rather than negatives. I constantly thank God for the husband he provided for me. Rich's tongue often saves him and defuses an uncomfortable scene, as he did with his mother's unkind words on that day so long ago. If he isn't encouraging me with positive ideas, he's doing something to refocus my hurt or anger toward something funny.

15) Keep accurate medical records; they are invaluable.

During the first year of Kathryn's life, we had weekly doctor appointments. After her head surgery, the appointments were changed to monthly visits for the next two years. Then they were changed to twice-yearly visits until she turned eight years old. I kept track of all doctor visits, procedures, medications, and surgeries, writing them down since there were too many to keep in my head. This proved to be valuable for later reference. The breakdown of her surgeries and illnesses follows:

In 1979, Kathryn had two seizures, the encephalocele collapsed; she was dehydrated with rectal bleeding. She had her head surgery to remove the encephalocele in December.

The following year, 1980, she was tested for hearing and vision. She had pneumonia at Christmas that year.

In 1981, she had right hip surgery and was in a full body cast for three weeks. Afterward she had extensive therapy. The Christmas season again brought pneumonia.

In 1982, she had left hip surgery and again a full body cast and extensive therapy.

The next three years brought more testing of her vision and hearing. Therapy was constantly being administered to keep her joints and muscles agile.

Again in 1986, she had surgery to release the Achilles tendon. She was in a cast for five weeks.

From 1987 until 1989, she was fine except for bladder and yeast infections.

In 1989, she had surgery on both heels and was in a full body cast for five weeks. Therapy was at the hospital in the care-by-parent unit three times a day for one week.

The next year brought more bladder and yeast infections. In October of 1990, she was diagnosed with Scoliosis. We took her to Shriners Hospital for a second opinion. Her spine curvature was at twenty degrees and surgery was not considered until it reached forty-five degrees. We decided that, if surgery was needed, it would be done at Shriners. By April of 1993, the curve was at twenty-eight degrees. During that same year, she had a wheelchair accident at school and lost her front tooth. She had a root canal and the dentist put the tooth back in place.

Miraculously, in October, 1993, Kathryn's curve was reduced to twenty-three degrees. Doctors still wanted to follow up, but changed the appointments to every other year. November that year brought on a mild case of chicken pox.

In January of 1996, the school called and said that Kathryn seemed very irritable. When she was dropped off at home that day, we agreed. We took her to the doctor, and he felt she had a bladder infection. However, there was no sign of infection, but the sugar in her urine was extremely high, and diabetes was suspected. We followed up the next day with a kidney specialist, and all the test results came out normal.

The following month, an x-ray revealed minor abnormalities in her bladder. Nothing significant resulted.

In October of 1997, she had two moles on her thigh removed. They were benign. She again went to Shriners Hospital in November of 1997. This time an x-ray revealed she had developed a second curve on the bottom of her spine that was the reverse of the one on top. The doctor said her spine was an "S" shape. Because of this new curve, her spine now was straighter and the doctor didn't think surgery would be necessary. She never had to go to Shriners again.

The next two years again brought yeast infections and strep throat. October just didn't seem to be her month, because during that month she developed stomach problems. Another x-ray revealed a tumor and possible obstruction in the gastric outlet. We took her to a specialist who recommended a scope diagnostic procedure to see what was in her stomach. The results of the test showed there was nothing, and the doctors were puzzled. What would show up on an x-ray, but be gone when they used a scope?

Kathryn continued to have urinary infections and started to be constipated more frequently. The doctors looked for another obstruction and another scope test was ordered. There was nothing found, however. The diagnosis was that her bowel was slowing down. He called it sluggish.

During these two years, Kathryn was experiencing a distended stomach. Sometimes it got so big it looked as if she was nine months pregnant. In May of 2002, I called Dr. Mangurten and asked for his opinion. He suggested we take Kathryn to a pediatric gastroenterologist for whom he had high regard. Dr. Mangurten set up this appointment as this doctor normally would not have taken her as a patient because her age classified her as an adult. The specialist diagnosed her with Aerophagia, the swallowing of her own air, which caused her stomach to expand. This was not a life-threatening illness. We found that by lying Kathryn on her stomach, the expansion would quickly go down.

Since 2002, Kathryn has been physically healthy. She hasn't even had a cold. She is doing exceptionally well for her condition and everyone is amazed when we tell them that she isn't on any medication.

Kathryn was diagnosed as multi-handicapped. She has microcephaly, she is legally blind, severely retarded, and also has cerebral palsy and cannot walk or talk.

When Kathryn was little, she wore a bonnet on her head at all times, even when she slept. We used her cute little bonnets for two reasons. It kept the bandages on the tumor in place so that we didn't have to put tape on her head. It also kept it from getting dirty and infected. With the bonnet on, Kathryn looked like any other "normal" child. It wasn't until she got older and needed a wheelchair that her disability became visible to those outside our family and core of close friends.

Ironically, by the time Kathryn was eight, she was able to stand and take a few steps with help. She could sit on the floor cross-legged, and get into that position by herself. She was also able to turn around in her bed. For some reason, all of this progress was lost after her last surgery in March of 1989. We are not sure what happened, but the therapist at school thought she was in the full body cast too long. She never moved her feet to walk, sit up, or turn over by herself again.

At first, the news that she would never walk disturbed Rich and me. We thought walking was essential for Kathryn, and she had worked so hard in therapy for ten years. Was all of her hard work in vain? As time went on, however, we realized that walking might have been dangerous for her. She was legally blind; she would not be able to see where she was walking. Because of her retardation, we wouldn't be able to protect her verbally if she walked into a dangerous situation. We would have to be constantly by her side to make sure she was safe. We realized God was protecting His child by taking away the ability to walk to keep her safe.

Contrary to what we were told by the physicians at her birth, instead of being a "vegetable in a fetal position the rest of her life," she is a charming, loving, gentle young lady. She can finger-feed herself. She understands simple requests such as, "Give me your hand. Give me a hug. Hold your glass."

Because her optic nerves were so small at birth, Kathryn was diagnosed as legally blind. How much she sees we will never know, because she can't tell us. We are convinced that she is able to see some things. She takes a glass held out to her without prompting. She reaches for a hand, with no verbal coaching. She reacts to closeness by touching someone in close proximity to her chair. Thankfully, she has exceeded expectations for social contact. Knowing she is aware of her surroundings encourages us to interact with her more often. Our close friends also pay attention to her for which we are thankful.

When we moved from one house to another, Kathryn was agitated for the first week. She makes two general sounds; one sounds happy and one sounds upset and bothered. She was groaning, using her discontented utterances. I couldn't understand why, but it finally occurred to me. She knew she was in a different house. I was concerned that she thought we were putting her into a nursing home facility to live without us. I decided to reassure her. "Kathryn, this is our new home. Daddy, you, and Mommy are going to live here. Don't be afraid. We're not going to leave you." She must have understood because she settled down immediately.

Kathryn repeatedly says, "I good girl," and once we were certain she asked for a cookie in the church nursery. When spoken to she responds with a sound. Her vocabulary has been limited. Although we don't really know how much she understands, we are convinced it is more than what we were originally led to believe. For now, it's enough for us to know she is not a vegetable, lying in a fetal position, oblivious to the whole world around her. That was the doctor's prognosis at birth.

The record of Kathryn's illnesses on my computer along with the dates, doctors in attendance, and results has been invaluable to me throughout the years. It accompanies me to all of Kathryn's doctor appointments and her respite services. Each time we place her in respite, dozens of pages must be filled out including her medical history. I am able to print a copy off the computer and attach it with the required paperwork. It's a great time saver. I highly recommend this kind of record keeping for any child, even more so for a child that has major medical needs. It's much easier to update a flowing record, than trying to create one looking back to past years.

Recently, I suggested to the directors of our two respite homes that it might be more prudent for them to computerize the 26–30 pages of forms that need to be filled out each time our daughter goes to one of their homes while we go away on vacation. By e-mailing the forms, it would save ink, paper, and postage. It would also be beneficial for parents, as in many cases, like ours, most of the required information does not change from year to year. Parents could fill out the forms once and update them as needed.

I have computerized all of these forms, and each year make necessary changes. What a time saver!

16) Real peace comes from God.

When Kathryn was eight years old, I attended a Catholic Church weekend retreat at St. Mary's College in South Bend, Indiana. It was a getaway for me after a difficult period.

A month earlier, I had been in Arizona to help my sister. She went off her medications and was paranoid and hallucinating. She needed to see a doctor and my dad gave me a hard time while I was trying to set up doctor appoints and get her the help she needed. He complained that the doctor I chose was too far away, which wasn't true, the doctor's office was less than three miles away. He complained that the appointment was too late in the afternoon, and he would have to drive back in rush hour. It was frustrating trying to work with a person that was so hard to please. I only had one week in Arizona and wanted to make sure that when I left, Pat was getting the help she needed. With all this frustration, I left Arizona angry. I told my parents I would never come back to see them again. I reasoned, my eight-year-old daughter was disabled, and there was nothing that I wouldn't do to get medical help for my little girl. My sister needed to see a doctor who would prescribe the right medications to get her back on track, and my parents weren't cooperating. I suppose that wasn't the only reason I was angry. Subconsciously, I resented my parents' lack of interest in my sister, my daughter, and myself through the years. This straw was the one that broke the camel's back.

Even at the time, I knew my words, thoughts, feelings, and actions were wrong. I shouldn't have talked to my parents the way I did. I knew forgiveness was in order, but I was at a loss as far as how to do that. For several months, anger raged within me. The timing was perfect when a friend from church invited me to the retreat. My heart was ready to receive what God was about to show me.

While at St. Mary's College, one of the priests suggested I read my Bible. When I returned home from the retreat, I eagerly grabbed my Bible and asked Rich to join me. We started with the book of Genesis in the Old Testament and had a hard time understanding what we read. Discouraged, we lost interest after a few chapters.

A week later, my car was having trouble, so I called my friend and mechanic Dennis to see if he could fix it. As I waited in his living room, I noticed that there was a Bible on an end table. Dennis' wife, Georgette, was keeping me company while Dennis worked on my car.

I shook my head and said, "I envy you; you know the Bible so well. Rich and I tried reading it, but it's too difficult. We couldn't understand it."

Georgette replied, pretty eagerly, "I would be glad to read the Bible with you. We'll start reading in the New Testament, though. It's easier to understand for a beginner."

I agreed, and we set a date to begin our study the following week.

When the appointed day rolled around, I almost forgot about our Bible study. Georgette called to confirm.

Thinking about my busy schedule, I tried to put my friend off. "Tomorrow?" I asked. "I was going to get some stuff done around here. I forgot about our lesson. Can we start next week instead?"

Georgette was ready for my excuses. "You aren't really serious about studying the Bible, are you?" She spoke kindly, but she was firm with me.

Her insinuation made me mad. I insisted I was serious. I was huffy when I answered, "Of course, I was serious. I just forgot."

I agreed to come to the study as originally planned. I was there on time and ready to study. After my verbal run-in with Georgette, I was going to prove I was responsible, reliable, and eager to learn.

The New Testament was much easier reading. Georgette and

I started in the Book of John. After the second lesson, I found what had been missing in my life: Jesus. That night I asked God to forgive me of all of my sins and asked Jesus into my heart. I believed He died *for me*. I believed He *had a special plan for my life,* and in the months and years that followed, He gradually revealed His plan to me.

When you receive Jesus into your heart, the Bible says you are born again, and that was true for me. I felt as if my life was starting over again. When I started reading more of the Bible, step-by-step, I saw God's plan for me. I had nothing to fear as long as I trusted and obeyed Him.

I grew up thinking I was a Christian, but I never really believed all that stuff about Jesus. A virgin birth? God's Son coming to earth, being tortured, and dying on a cross for me? Who in their right mind could believe all that? I did love Christmas, and all the presents and parties. Easter wasn't so bad either, with getting time off from school and another party with great food. So, I went along with the game plan. After all, I believed in God. Wasn't that good enough? Why did I have to believe in Jesus too?

One of the challenges in my life has been low self-esteem. I looked for approval from my parents, family and friends…always seeking to be, but never feeling as if I was good enough. Fear and worry ruled in my mind. As an adult, now married for a second time, I worried about Rich. What if he lost his job? I worried about Kathryn dying, and worried more about her living. I was afraid I'd never be able to raise this child as she got bigger and I got older. I worried about who would take care of her if I died. I even worried about nuclear war, the hole in the o-zone layer, and greenhouse gases. Peace was not an option in anything. I feared that God was not only picking on me with all the trials in my life, but that He must actually hate me. I would ask myself, "Why did

God hate me so much? And, if he didn't hate me, then why did He allow all this suffering in my life?" I questioned God over and over again.

As I was reading my Bible one morning, I came across John 9:1–3: *"And as He passed by, He saw a man blind from birth. And His disciples asked Him, saying, 'Rabbi, who sinned, this man or his parents, that he should be born blind?' Jesus answered, 'It was neither that this man sinned, nor his parents; but it was in order that the works of God might be displayed in him.'"* For the first time since Kathryn was born, I finally understood why God gave me a disabled daughter. He wasn't punishing me for my sins. He didn't hate me. He loved me very much. He knew that by giving me a disabled daughter I would get involved in disability ministry. I could never do that if I didn't experience what it takes to raise a disabled daughter. I not only would not have any interest in such a ministry, but I wouldn't be able to relate to another mother with a disabled child if my daughter was healthy. This was His plan for our family, and day by day, it became clearer.

Little by little, the fear and worry was transformed as I gave my life and heart over to a higher power…Jesus. With Him as the pilot of my life, I know that every trial I'd been through God uses so that I can help others through similar problems. I have been able to comfort women who have been raised by an alcoholic father or an insensitive mother. Because of my divorce, I related to Rich's cousin as he went through similar struggles. I became his support system because he knew I truly understood what he was going through.

Because my brother killed himself, I have been able to talk and encourage people who have lost a loved one to suicide. Besides, who is more capable of being a support system to parents of newborn disabled children than a person who has walked in those moccasins?

Years later, as I drew closer to God, He gave me peace and showed me how Richard and I needed to trust Him with every part of our life.

Rich came home from work looking worried.

I questioned him, "What's wrong, Honey?"

"Nothing," he replied quite unconvincingly.

I could tell he wasn't being truthful, so again I pushed for the truth. "Please tell me what's wrong. I can see on your face you are worried about something. Please don't hide it from me."

Confronted by me once more he confessed. "I don't want to worry you, but the company is doing cut backs and I might lose my job," he replied.

"That's okay, God will find you another one," came my unexpected answer.

Rich looked at me as if he was seeing an alien from outer space. For years, he heard me agonizing over less serious problems. This response was so out of character for me. He knew I had changed and finally had peace in my life. He wanted to have that same peace in his own life. I don't remember the exact time, but sometime shortly after this conversation, Rich received Jesus into his heart. He now understands the dramatic change that simple step of faith makes in a man's life.

To my amazement, the more I submit my will to God's will, the more He shows me *THE PLAN*. As God slowly reveals His plan for my life, the more I see how much He really loves me. As I look back at my whole life, I see how God protects and watches over me. The story Erma Bombeck concluded her second article with about the footprints in the sand was written specifically for me.

Through the years, people have said they admire Richard and me for how we have accepted and cared for Kathryn. They usually continued to say they could never do what we're doing. I assure them, "It's not us. We're only human. The credit goes to God. If someone had told me thirty-one years ago that I would have a disabled daughter and I would accept this and minister to others in similar circumstances, I would have told them they were crazy. It's only by God's amazing grace that we have made it to this point."

During my pregnancy, I asked the doctor for an amniocentesis test. He refused to give me that test saying it was dangerous for the fetus. Since my pregnancy had been uneventful to that point, he could see no reason to give it to me. If he had consented, I would have known early on that Kathryn would be born with severe problems. Would I have opted for an abortion? I honestly can't say what I would have done. I thank God that He protected me from knowing and possibly making the worst decision of my life. I shudder to think I might have aborted our beautiful daughter who has brought us so much love and happiness.

In the book, *How Would Jesus Vote* by Dr. James Kennedy and Jerry Newcombe, the authors wrote about the affects of abortion on the women who had the procedure. They said, "The task force paid special attention to two thousand women who had abortions, concluding, 'Of these post-abortive women, over 99 percent of them testified that abortion is destructive of the rights, interests, and health of women and that abortion should not be legal.'"

We should feel sorry for women who have aborted their unborn children. They will never know the wonderful plan God had for that little life and will live with guilt for the rest of their lives unless they receive Christ and learn that Jesus' death on the cross takes away the burden of the sin they bear.

Before I invited Jesus into my life, I read a book on how to have better self-esteem. In the few pages I read, the author said the solution to improving one's ego was by growing closer to God through reading the Bible and trusting the Lord. I scoffed that I'd thought this book would answer my questions. Instead, I figured it was a lot of religious propaganda and "hocus pocus." I was disappointed because I'd hoped the book would have some practical advice. How wrong I was. I had stumbled onto the answers and I didn't recognize the truth when it stared me in the face.

In contrast to what I thought before I found Christ, I learned after accepting Him into my life that Jesus Christ is the answer to all of life's problems. As Kathryn grew, her problems multiplied, and I had to turn to God over and over again because the doctors couldn't help me. Jesus never let me down. He didn't always solve my problems, but He gave me peace about them. He didn't always change the situation, but He changed my attitude toward it. He gave me faith, in Him and in myself.

We have a Global Positioning System (GPS) in our car. One lovely summer day we were invited to our friend's summer home on a lake in Wisconsin. We decided to use the GPS. The system took us a different route than we had previously taken. At one point, it directed us down a side road and the bridge was out. There were detour signs all over, so we had to turn around. After recalculating, our faithful GPS gave us new directions. Sure enough, within a few minutes, we arrived at our destination.

It takes faith to trust this small mechanical box, yet we completely believe in this talking device. The Bible is God's GPS for our lives. It directs us on the path that God designed in His plan. Sometimes He, too, throws in a detour to direct us in some new way. Just like the car's GPS system, it takes a lot of faith to believe we will arrive safely at our divine destination with God as our pilot. What is faith? Webster's Dictionary says that faith is believing something we cannot prove. Sadly, today people put more faith into their automobile's Global Positioning System than they do in the Bible. Jesus said in John 14:6, *"I am the way, the truth, and the life; no one comes to the Father, but through Me."* The GPS can get you to your earthly destination, but Jesus Christ will guide you safely to an eternal home in heaven.

My father was ill for many years while I was growing up. He often said, "If you have your health, you have everything." He repeated and repeated this and I came to believe his words. Then one day I was talking to my friend, Georgette, and I quoted my dad. She looked at me strangely and said, "I don't believe that." Her comment surprised me, and I asked how anyone could not agree with that.

She was quick to respond. "I believe that peace is more important than good health. A lot of people that have good health are unhappy because they don't have any peace. On the other hand, some people who are ill have a large measure of peace, and they are happy."

At the time, I didn't know the peace Georgette was talking about. It isn't the peace as in "no war on the earth," as the world thinks of peace. It is the peace that comes only from our Lord, Jesus Christ.

Jesus said, *"Peace I leave with you; My peace I give you; not as the world gives; do I give to you. Let not your heart be troubled, nor let it be fearful"* (John 14:27).

The peace Georgette was referring to was the peace in Philippians 4:7:

> *"And the peace of God, which surpasses all comprehension, shall guard your hearts and your minds in Christ Jesus."*

True peace comes when we receive Jesus into our hearts. I have personally experienced this peace in my life, so I know this is true.

17) Parents of healthy children have problems, too.

When Kathryn was young, it was difficult for me to observe children her age walking, talking, and playing. Kathryn had to be held and carried in my arms at the age of two and three. She was not walking and talking like the other two and three year olds, and she certainly was not able to play as other toddlers. I shed tears. I had fears. I had many, many questions.

It was with the help we received from professionals at the hospital, Dr. Mangurten, the professionals at Julia Molloy and Shore, the schools Kathryn attended, dear friends and family, and coming into a personal relationship with Jesus that life was tolerable.

It wasn't until years later when Kathryn and all my friends' children got into their teen years when I realized that having a disabled child wasn't so bad. As we watched what other parents of teens were enduring, I began to think I preferred the way Kathryn was.

That preference was confirmed through several experiences. One incident occurred when we were going on vacation to California. I decided to go to Kids R Us to buy Kathryn new outfits for the trip. I got to the store and found eight outfits I could mix-and-match. *That will take care of packing for her,* I thought. I went to pay for the clothes and stood in a line behind a woman with her eight-year old daughter. Her daughter was giving her a hard time because she couldn't get another outfit she *really, really* wanted. The mother saw me put down my purchases and asked, "Do you mind if I ask who you're buying those outfits for?"

I smiled, predicting in my mind where the conversation was headed, then answered, "We're planning a trip to California, and these are for my daughter. There were so many good sales; I decided to buy more than I came for."

"How old is your daughter?" the woman asked.

"She's eight."

The mother was surprised. She said, "She's eight years old, and she lets you pick out her clothes? My daughter would never let me do that. If I did, she probably wouldn't wear them."

I nodded. "My daughter is severely retarded; she doesn't walk or talk, so she can't pick out her own clothes."

The woman looked sympathetically at me. Tears welled as she said, "I'm terribly sorry. How hard it must be for you."

I was careful to be positive and yet grateful for her caring words. "She's a happy little girl and easy to care for. From what I see, I think you have it harder with your daughter."

"What do you mean?" She looked at me incredulously.

"My daughter won't complain about what I bought. She'll wear these outfits and be content."

She understood what I was saying, and we both laughed as we left the store.

Richard and I have never had to cope with a child using drugs, dealt with teenage drinking problems, worried about our daughter getting into a car accident, or paced the floor when she'd stayed out past her curfew. We've always known where Kathryn is at night. We didn't have to scrimp and save for her college education. We didn't have to plan and put money in our bank account for a lavish wedding.

I'm not trying to be flippant, but parents of healthy children have problems, too. Even when children marry, and you think that they are finally out on their own, you might get a surprise. Many grandparents today are raising their grandchildren because of divorce or illness.

18) Don't make or ask for promises that can't be kept.

When Kathryn graduated from Julia Molloy, we were the only parents who had arranged for a special needs trust and guardianship for our special needs child. When a child turns eighteen, they are considered to be of legal age and able to make their own decisions. The law doesn't change for a disabled child no matter how severely retarded. So, unless the parents claim legal guardianship, the state has the right to take over the child's care. It was important to us that we, not the government, make important decisions for Kathryn.

When we were working out the Special Needs Trust for Kathryn with our lawyer, the decisions weren't easy. There were questions such as, "Who do you trust with your child's life? What if the guardians you appoint get sick? What if they die before your child?" These came up regularly in our counseling sessions as we drew up the legal documents. With the help of our attorney and lots of prayer, we had peace of mind about Kathryn's future though it was overwhelming at the start.

Two sets of guardians should be chosen in case the primary custodians cannot fulfill this obligation. Richard and I chose family members to stand as Kathryn's primary guardians. We discussed the options with them. Keeping Kathryn at home would be our first choice; however, we gave them flexibility to reverse that decision if their situation changed. If keeping her in the home became impossible or too difficult, we released them from their obligation and commitment. All we asked of them was that if they needed to place our daughter in a home, they make certain she was safe and her needs were being met.

Richard once promised that if something happened to me that he would continue to care for Kathryn at home after I was gone or could no longer shoulder my share of her care. I would not accept his promise. If I died and Rich wanted to remarry, his promise would commit a second wife to his obligation. That hardly seemed fair to another woman, nor was it a forecast for a happy marriage. If Rich's physical condition prevented him from caring for Kathryn, he might also need to change his mind. I didn't want either of us to feel guilty for breaking an impossible promise. Regardless of all of this, if Kathryn outlives one or both of us, I am persuaded that God will continue to care for her as He has during her first thirty years.

19) God loves your child more than you do.

Through the years, several people have suggested that we put Kathryn into a skilled care home. They were concerned because we're getting older, and these homes all have long waiting lists. "Don't you need to put her on a list?" I was asked many times. We were not ready to do that, yet we had questions that needed answers. What if one of us did get sick? How would the other person be able to care for two sick people? What if one of us died? I can barely lift Kathryn from her wheelchair to her bed now. How would I be able to do that alone? I believe that God knew my doubts, and He, in the midst of all my uncertainty, gave me peace of mind.

A few years ago, a family with a disabled daughter attended our church. They had three daughters, two bright, healthy girls and one, Laura, who was severely disabled. She was on feeding tubes, had seizures, and needed constant care, day and night. It was hard on the family and especially for their other two school-aged daughters. When Laura awoke sick during the night, the whole family was up.

I made a suggestion to Pat. "Have you ever looked into respite so you and the rest of the family could get away for a little while by yourselves?"

She was interested, but didn't know anything about such a plan. She asked, "How would I go about getting respite?"

We talked and I gave her the number for respite at Misericordia. Their family decided to try a weekend to see how things went. Pat carried a beeper with her in case of an emergency. The weekend went smoothly.

A few months went by and Pat called me again. She explained that she and her husband were thinking of putting Laura into a permanent living situation at Misericordia. It was getting harder on the whole family.

This would be a difficult decision since the two daughters were like "little moms" to Laura. They loved her and helped with her care a great deal. The decision was difficult on the whole family, but to go ahead with permanent care in a skilled home was a wise move for them.

I knew their situation was different from ours. Kathryn is an only child; they had other children who needed attention. Pat called saying, "I called Misericordia today to see if we could put Laura in full time. They said there was a six-year waiting list. I was surprised. I didn't expect that. But they're going to send me an application and put her on the list. I guess I'd better start the process now since it takes so long."

About a month went by and I got a call from Pat. She surprised me again when she said, "Please pray for me. I'm in shock.

Misericordia called me today and said that two children had passed away, and they can take Laura immediately. They told me to bring her right in." Then after an uneasy pause, she added, "I'm not sure I'm ready for this."

God knew their family was struggling, so He opened doors for them. That was my answer from God, too. I knew right then and there if God wanted Kathryn in a nursing home, He would get her into one when He knew it was time.

God showed me through this situation and others that He will take over Kathryn's care when I cannot do it. For years, I worried about how I would be able to be with my parents and my best friend, Kay, if they were to get sick with a long illness. I had Kathryn to take care of, yet I couldn't imagine not being there when Mom, Dad, or Kay needed me the most. I prayed that God would not allow them to have a prolonged illness or be so sick they needed a lot of care. I prayed that if it was their time to die, He would take them home quickly. It was not just for my benefit that I prayed this way. No one wants to see their loved ones suffer.

God was gracious. My father died on May 6, 1990. He came downstairs that morning and was waiting on the sofa for my mother to finish making breakfast. He died on the sofa, still waiting for his bacon and eggs.

My best friend in California, Kay, enjoyed good health until she got pneumonia. Since she had pneumonia several years earlier and came through it okay, I debated whether I should fly out and be with her. I was working at church when Ann, our pastor's wife, came in. I told her about my dilemma. She said, "You go." I had a feeling in my heart this was a direct order from God. I made my flight arrangements. The Lord took Kay home less than two weeks later, and I was able to see her and spend time with her before she died.

My mother was diagnosed with lung cancer in May of 2004. It was her third and last bout with the disease. After she was diagnosed, I decided to retire from my church position as Administrative Assistant so I could spend more time with her. I made five trips to Arizona in the two and a half years before her death. During this time, she functioned so well we thought she had been mis-diagnosed. She exercised every day, ate well, and seemed to be in great spirits. I was privileged to lead my mother to the Lord in February of 2006, just months before she died.

In November of 2006, Mom was rushed to the hospital. She was having difficulty breathing. I flew out to be with her at the hospice facility. At first, she was afraid. She didn't want to die. She asked me not to leave her. I asked the nursing staff if I could have a cot and sleep next to my mom. They cooperated and brought in a cot just before bedtime. Several times during the next three nights, my mom awoke with anxiety attacks as her breathing labored. I held her hand and assured her that Jesus would get her through this trial. Her fear turned into resignation as she finally welcomed death and eternal happiness with Jesus. She died less than two weeks after she entered the hospice unit.

The doctors said that Rich's mother could have survived for months in a coma after the aneurysm in her head burst. We moved her to our home for hospice knowing that God was well aware of what we could, or could not, handle. God's timing was again perfect. The week Rich's mother was moved into our home for hospice, Rich already had the week off. He needed to take his last week of vacation or lose it, so he took those seven days. I was still working at the church only two blocks away from home.

I went home at lunchtime to check on Rich and Mom. Her last day, I came home and found the doctor there. He indicated that it wouldn't be long, possibly only a couple hours. I called Rich's sister to let her know. Within the hour, she, her husband, and her daughter arrived. Grandma hung on until Kathryn came home from school. Rich took Kathryn off the bus and began to lay her in bed. I told Rich, "Bring Kathryn in to say goodbye to Grandma." He did. I then said, "Grandma, Kathryn's here to say goodbye to you." It was as if she was waiting for the whole family to be together, because right after I said that, she took her last breath and died. It was Friday, the last day of Rich's vacation. God knew that her surviving longer would have created a hardship for all of us.

Our friend, Josie, was diagnosed with terminal breast cancer. She had one daughter, Brenda, who was married and had children. She knew that after she died Brenda would be okay with her family surrounding her. She was more concerned about her dog, Cuddles. Brenda had a dog and would not be able to care for another one. Distressed, she would comment, "Cuddles always met me at the front door when I came home from work. What's going to happen to her when I die?" What happened next reassured me that God cares about everything, even His four-legged creatures. Cuddles died one week before Josie, alleviating Josie's worries about her beloved dog. This also showed me that one way or another, God would take care of Kathryn if Rich and I couldn't. Matthew 6:26 tells us, *"Look at the birds of the air, that they do not sow, neither do they reap, nor gather into barns, yet your heavenly Father feeds them. Are you not worth more than they?"*

The one thing that I desire my readers glean from this book more than anything else is how much God loves you. When you realize how important you are to Him, your life will change drastically for the better.

20) God allows what is best for you.

Christians can talk to God, their heavenly father, about any decisions or problems. I pray about everything. People smile and ask if I really think God cares about my broken car. Yes, I believe God does care about each and every detail of our lives. The Bible says that God cares for the birds in the air and the flowers of the field, so why wouldn't He care about all my problems?

The night before our wedding, Rich called about the weather forecast for our special day. He was concerned, saying, "Honey, it's going to rain tomorrow."

"It won't rain on my wedding day," I said.

Rich was sympathetic. He said, "I know you're disappointed, but the weatherman said, 'Rain all day.'"

I adamantly said, "I don't care what the weatherman said. It will not rain on my wedding day."

April 9, 1978 was a beautiful, sunny day, unusually warm for early April in Illinois. It never rained that day, and to this day Rich believes that I can control the weather, or that I have an "IN" with the Rainmaker. He might just be right about that!

Once, while in California visiting my friend Kay, I noticed a can on her counter that had the words "GOD CAN" in bold letters. The can felt light as if it was empty. I asked her about it.

She smiled and explained. "Honey, every time I have a problem that I can't solve I write it down on a piece of paper and put it in the can. Then I pray and ask God to fix it."

"But why the can? Why not just pray about it?" I asked.

"The can reminds me what I can't fix, GOD CAN," Kay concluded.

She was a sincere Christian. She rarely worried about things she couldn't control. She would always take it to the Lord in prayer. She had enormous faith in God. The Bible tells us not to ask God for anything if we don't believe that He will provide. Our starting point is faith.

The right thing to do may not always be obvious, so God has given us His book of instructions, the Bible. When I question, "What should I do?" I get answers either by reading the Bible or praying. James 1:5-6 says, *"If any of you lacks wisdom, let him ask of God, who gives to all men generously and without reproach, and it will be given to him. But let him ask in faith without any doubting, for the one who doubts is like the surf of the sea driven and tossed by the wind. For let not that man expect that he will receive anything from the Lord."* Do you trust God to do what's best for you?

21) There are two words that can save your marriage.

Like most married couples, Rich and I have had our share of disagreements in thirty-one years of marriage. When we analyzed these arguments, we realized that most of them were just differences of opinion. So why were these discussions getting so heated? We are both individuals with a right to different opinions. So, several years ago we came up with a solution to these worthless arguments. When a discussion was lasting too long, and we could see that neither one of us was about to budge or agree with the other, one of us says, "Cancel! Cancel!" When these words are expressed by one or the other party, we immediately stop the discussion and change the subject. If one of us tries to get in the last word, the other repeats "Cancel! Cancel!" and that ends the argument.

If you are angry and hurt because of something that was said pointedly at you, then "Cancel! Cancel!" will not work. These words are not appropriate when your spouse has hit below the belt or said something mean to you. You need to support your spouse and assure them that they are valuable, being sensitive to their emotional needs. There are two other words that are necessary and work much better. They are, "I'm Sorry!"

PART SIX

No Man Is an Island

A man of many friends comes to ruin,

but there is a friend who sticks closer than a brother.

PROVERBS 18:24

There are four Kathryns who have impacted my life. Although they all spelled their names differently, the four Kathryns share similar attributes. They are survivors; they didn't give up when trials came into their lives. The name "Kathryn" means strong, and the four of them are strong in so many ways.

The first Katherine in my life was my grandmother on my father's side. In 1912, my grandmother, who we called Busia, came to America when she was only thirteen years old with one year of formal schooling. In a couple of years, she could read, write, and speak English. She worked cleaning office buildings earning ten cents an hour in downtown Chicago. She saved money from her meager income to send home each month to help out the family in Poland. In 1916, at the age of seventeen, she married my grandfather, Stanley. They worked hard and saved their money so they could buy the tavern where they made their fortune. My dad was her firstborn. When dad was eight years old, Busia had her second son, Stanley. He had complications at birth and died the next day. My grandmother never spoke of Stanley to me until our Kathryn was born. Once Busia had her third child, my aunt Bernice, she was able to move on with her life. Kathryn's birth and the possibility of the death of her great granddaughter brought up sad memories that had been eclipsed by happier times.

By the early 1920s, my grandparents amassed a small fortune, purchased the building that housed their tavern and sixteen apartments, and became landlords along with running their business. They lived in another house they owned several blocks from their business. Life was going well for them. Busia made a trip to Poland to visit her family and the relatives she had been supporting for years. It was a happy reunion. I learned years later while I visited my dad's cousin, Celina, in Krakow that while Busia was in Poland she bought washing machines for every relative left in the old country. The appliance was considered a great luxury for a family in Poland at that time.

My grandparents were doing well until the Great Depression of 1933 hit the United States. During this same year, my grandmother gave birth to her third child, my Aunt Bernice. I can't imagine how hard it must have been for her, taking care of her newborn while struggling with the financial turmoil of trying to keep their business and properties. They lost everything, including their home and the building where the business was located. However, they managed to hold on to the tavern, renting the space, and began saving money again. After a few years, they'd earned enough to afford two more houses and a farm, planning to retire in the country.

When my car was stolen in 1978, Busia encouraged me with her story about the Great Depression. "People killed themselves when they lost everything. How stupid. It was only money; your life is worth more than all the money in the world. You can always get more money, but you only have one life." With lessons like this, she taught me to be a survivor, too.

Busia had a keen business sense. When I was in high school,

she went to Poland for a visit. At that time, Poland was still under communist rule. It was customary to ask someone going back to Poland to deliver money to their family. Money sent through the mail would never reach the people for whom it was intended. The communists would confiscate it, or the postal workers would steal it. It was difficult to send financial support to family when the government made it impossible.

Concerned relatives got around the difficulty by sending money via Polish visitors willing to hand deliver their gifts. Several people came to the house to give Busia money. While in Poland, she visited each family and gave them their monetary gift. About a month after she returned from Poland, one of the women who had given her money came over. She was angry. "I got a letter from my brother in Poland today. He said you never gave him the money. You stole my money, and I want it back."

I was appalled. My grandmother was completely honest. As teenagers, my sister Pat and I lived with Busia after my parents moved to Arizona. Her sense of honesty made her a model of integrity to the two of us. More often than I could remember, her example of honesty was modeled to us.

One incident occurred during the blizzard of January 1967, which left twenty-six inches of snow covering the city of Chicago. Our street was one of the few streets to be plowed. We were fortunate there was road construction going on just before the storm hit. The construction company collected ten dollars from each house on the street and cleared the snow all the way to the main thoroughfare which had been plowed by the city. We were among the few residents that could get around the city within a day after the storm.

The sidewalks, however, weren't cleared for several weeks. As I left for work that day, Busia asked me to pick up a loaf of white

bread on my way home. Busia was less than five feet tall and
heavyset. The snow was deeper than she was tall. A trip to the
local grocery store only two blocks away would have been impossible for her. I came home with the bread and gave it to her. She
handed me a quarter and said, "I don't have a penny. I'll pay you
when I get one." I argued, saying I didn't want the money. She
was generous with my sister and me, charging us only ten dollars
a week for room and board. Though Pat and I didn't know it,
she saved all of this money in separate savings accounts for each
of us. When we went out on our own, she added money to the
accounts and gave us each three thousand dollars. Several days
after I brought home that loaf of bread, she came to me with
the penny she said she still owed me. She was as honest as they
came.

Knowing the honesty of my grandmother, not even willing to
cheat someone out of a penny, I could not believe that she would
ever take anything that didn't belong to her. I waited for her to
say something to this woman. Instead, she got up without a word
and went upstairs to her room. Neither the woman nor I could
imagine what she was doing. I wondered why she wasn't defend-
ing herself against the accusation.

A couple of minutes later she returned. Without a word, she
handed the lady a piece of paper, and I could see it embarrassed
the Polish woman. It was a receipt for the money, signed by her
brother. The woman couldn't apologize enough. I could only
imagine what she would say to her brother in her next letter.

My mother's brother, Uncle Eddie, was indebted to Busia,
who was no relation to him. After marrying his wife, Virginia,
he wanted to build a home for her and their family, but he had
never purchased anything on credit. Since he had paid cash for
everything, the bank would not finance a loan. Busia loaned him

money to build that first house. From then until the day he died, he gave credit to my grandmother for his financial success. He said, "I wouldn't have anything today if your grandmother hadn't trusted me." When he died on October 16, 1996, he owned three homes in Arkansas, Oklahoma, and Mexico.

Busia was less than five feet tall and weighed about one hundred and seventy pounds. She ate fried meats, sauerkraut, and potatoes for breakfast, a habit learned in Poland. Any doctor or nutritionist would not recommend her diet today. However, she enjoyed good health all her life, except for a slightly elevated blood pressure for which she took garlic capsules, not traditional medications. When she died on December 19, 1982 at age 83, she had all her own teeth and a sharp mind. She delivered her children at home, so her first and only hospitalization was for one week just before she died. Busia spent a minimum of one hour a day praying in her bedroom. She valued her health above money. She used her money wisely and gave freely to those in need. She was known for her generosity to her family and friends, her sense of fairness, her honesty, and her inner strength. Growing up I made a conscious decision to be like my grandmother. She was my mentor, and I loved her dearly.

CHAPTER TWENTY-SIX

The second Kathryn in my life was my best friend, Kathryn Hager. I met Kay the year I was divorced from Lennie. He left me with nothing and I was struggling to get my life and finances together.

I marvel at how Kay and I met and became good friends in a remarkably short time. She was the executive secretary to Mr. Horberg, co-owner of Dynascan where I worked. Shortly after I began working at Dynascan, another friend from work, Donna, told me Kay had invited us over for dinner, and Kay wouldn't take "no" for an answer. Kay backed up Donna's invitation by calling me at my desk with her personal invitation in a voice that was more commanding than inviting. A woman in her sixties, she looked very intimidating to me with a cigarette dangling from her mouth, sitting at her desk outside Mr. Horberg's office. I would never have guessed we would become unparalleled friends for the next twenty-seven years.

Though years apart in age, I quickly learned that Kay and I had lots in common. She was a gourmet cook and loved the theater and musicals. She loved going on short day trips to Wisconsin, Long Grove, and almost any shopping center. She shopped. I looked. We always had fun together.

There were many dinners at her condo. She had divorced her first two alcoholic husbands and lost her third, loving husband to cancer. She knew my loneliness; she had experienced my loss. She could relate to me as no one else.

Often on Fridays after work Kay picked me up at my apartment, and we'd go to her condo for dinner, swimming, and a weekend outing. We usually spent the whole weekend together. She had good taste and liked only the finest restaurants. Determined not to be a freeloader, I never allowed her to treat me, so I usually picked the most inexpensive meal on the menu. Kay loved life, and I loved Kay. She became my surrogate mother.

After we'd worked together for several months, Donna, my friend and the Assistant Personnel Manager at Dynascan, asked me if I would like to go to Florida with her to visit her parents. She planned to move to California and wanted to make a trip to Florida to see her parents before she left. I saved every penny so I could make the trip. About a week before we were supposed to go, Donna said she'd decided not to go to Florida. Her funds were getting low, and she wasn't sure she could afford the trip. I was disappointed, but I decided to give my grandmother the money I'd saved for the trip as an extra payment on the loan for the Ford Mustang she financed for me. Unbelievably, someone had stolen my ten-year-old divorce settlement, "Clunker," right out from underneath my window. It was a low blow for me. No car meant a two-mile walk or taking three buses to get to work. Thank God for Kay! She picked me up and took me to work until I got my new Mustang.

I no sooner gave my grandmother the extra money and Donna called me at work saying she'd changed her mind and was going to go to Florida after all. I was so disappointed. Regretfully, I said there was no way I could go since I no longer had the money. In little more than a half-hour, Kay called me into her office. She handed me a check for three hundred dollars, enough money for airfare and other expenses. She said this trip was a chance of a lifetime for me and reminded me it would be inexpensive because I had a free place to stay. I could pay her back whenever I got the money, but she wanted me to go. I argued that I didn't believe in borrowing money for a vacation, but she insisted. When I got back to my desk, I wrote her an I.O.U. for three hundred dollars and marched right back to her desk. She ripped it up saying, "Honey, if I didn't trust you, I wouldn't have given you the check in the first place." I couldn't believe that someone I had known for such a short time would have such confidence in me. Her confidence bonded our friendship even more.

Kay reminded me of a socialite. She always dressed up. She didn't have "around the house" clothes and "going out" clothes. She always dressed in her finest clothes and jewelry, even while cooking gourmet meals. This was foreign to the way I was raised. We had "good" clothes and "play/work" clothes. We had to change the minute we got home from school into our "play/work" clothes.

As my "second mom," I could always count on Kay for godly wisdom and encouragement, unlike my real mother. I loved my mother, but she was stuck in yesterday. Although born in the United States and a U.S. citizen, she returned to Poland with her parents when she was about two years old. She dwelt on all the unhappiness she endured during her youth on the farm in Poland. Being the second child and oldest daughter, as she got older and her mother became ill, she took on more and more of the responsibility of raising her seven younger siblings. Mom had chores on the farm and life was hard. She became bitter that her parents didn't stay in America and that she lost opportunities other American children had growing up in the United States. As an American citizen, she also felt cheated out of a good education that would have given her better life choices. Instead, her lack of education meant working for minimum wage the rest of her life.

Mom returned to America on June 20, 1938 at the age of eighteen in the midst of the Great Depression. She married my father at twenty, and had her first child the day before her first wedding anniversary. Under those circumstances, attending school in America was impossible. My father was an alcoholic and marrying him added to her depression and unhappiness. So when my daughter was born and went through five surgeries and several hospitalizations, it was Kay, not my mother, that I turned to for emotional support. She always had the right words to say. I could count on her.

Kay's happiness wasn't due to a trouble-free life. Her father was also an alcoholic and died when she was young. She had to quit high school and go to work to support her widowed mother and herself. Providing for her mother was not a sacrifice, however, because she loved her, and it was what she wanted to do. She went through three marriages, each with issues and problems. Although I met her in Chicago as Kay, her family and friends in California called her "Molly," a nickname given to her by her grandmother. I never called her Molly, but after seeing Debbie Reynolds in "The Unsinkable Molly Brown," I could see the comparison of Kay to Molly. She was, in my opinion, totally unsinkable.

She also had a great sense of humor. Shortly after Rich and I got married, Rich told Kay that since he married me, we had a lot more mail coming in from places he never heard from before; Sears, J.C. Penny's, Marshall Fields, Carson's, Discover Card, and Visa Card. Kay laughed and without any hesitation she said, "Honey, don't you know that it's your job to earn money and

Barb's job to spend it? She can't help it if she's doing a better job than you are."

Like my grandmother, Kay enjoyed good health and had an amazing memory up until her death on November 16, 2004, at ninety-two. Kay, as her name suggests, was strong, wise, and godly. In the twenty-seven years of our friendship, harsh words never passed between us. She hated living alone but never complained. When she felt lonely, she did a good deed for someone. Throughout her life, she took in people who needed a place to stay when they were down and out. As she got older and her friends criticized her for doing this saying she couldn't handle the extra stress and work, she simply answered, "If there's room in your heart, there is room in your home."

She never felt sorry for herself. When she had pain from arthritis, she would say, "I can be at home and in pain, or I can go out and have pain. So let's go out and have some fun." She busily cooked gourmet meals and fed half the people in her church and neighborhood. Under her tutelage, I learned to cook and serve lovely meals, appreciate plays and operas, and enjoy life to the fullest. When I needed advice or words of encouragement, I could always count on her. She was a lady and someone I admired. She was God sent, and I miss her dearly.

CHAPTER TWENTY-SEVEN

The third Catherine who has impacted my life is my sister in the Lord, Catherine Fink. Her friendship and help has been priceless, and for the past decade, I don't know what I would do without her. She is the most loving, caring, helpful friend anyone could hope for. She, too, has her own special story.

Raised in an affluent area in the city of Chicago, Cate's mother knew of the finer things in life. She was from high society; her father, Cate's grandfather, was an entrepreneur. Everything he touched turned to gold. Not only was he successful in America, but he owned valuable property in Germany as well. Unfortunately, as a teenager, Cate's mother developed a heart problem after a bout with the flu. She married an Evanston fireman and relocated to that northern Chicago suburb often referred to as part of the exclusive "North Shore." Cate was the youngest of four children, and their life was comfortable though her mother's "socialite" status faded.

Growing up, neither Cate nor her sister, Jean, knew of their mother's heart condition. "Mom was happy and never complained, so when she lost her breath climbing stairs, we never gave it a second thought," Cate said. "We were given many household chores to do because Mom couldn't do them. We didn't think

213

much of it. We figured she was training us for future responsibilities when we married."

Born in 1930, Cate was raised during the Depression. Times were difficult for families, especially for the children who didn't understand world events. Cate remembers one of her teachers in school required the class to recite the following verse:

"Use it up,
Wear it out,
Make it do,
Or do without."

To this day, Cate is excellent at handling her finances. Though she watches her money, she is also generous to her family, friends, and charities.

Cate's mom died in 1956 when Cate was twenty-six years old. Her dad remarried in 1968, and he died in 1970. Cate married Robert Fink on November 15, 1952. Like Cate, Bob has a genuine love and heart for disabled people. When Cate is unable to help with Kathryn, Bob is quick to volunteer. Before Cate and Bob got involved with our family, they ministered to another family with a disabled daughter. They are always available to help us. They, and their five children, have become family to Rich, Kathryn, and me.

Like the other two Kates in my life, Cate Fink lives up to her name and is independent, strong, and never feels sorry for herself, nor does she dwell on unpleasant memories. She is a positive, joyful person. She is grateful for everything she has and counts everything in her life as a blessing. She loves to quote an old American proverb: "Love many, trust few, always paddle your own canoe."

Cate is content with the life God has given her and doesn't

consider money of major importance. She says, "My greatest riches are in the five wonderful children we've raised. We're very close." It has been a privilege for Rich, Kathryn, and me to be included in the Fink family.

I've learned many lessons from Cate. She taught me to let go of people who don't care about me. Her philosophy makes sense, as no one's destiny is tied to those who have left and gone their own way. That's our past, and there is a great new future awaiting us. She has also taught me to let go of things that aren't important, not to sweat the small stuff, that real friendship comes from mutual trust and love, and that true friendship is a gift from God.

CHAPTER TWENTY-EIGHT

God has put wonderful family members into my life like my Aunt Bernice and her husband, Chester. While I was growing up, Cocia (this means aunt in Polish and is what I always called her) lived in the same building as my family. She was ten years older than me, and I always thought of her more like a sister than an aunt. She went to my graduation from high school when my dad was sick and my mom had to stay at home with him. She stuck by me through the divorce from Lennie, and encouraged me when I married Rich. We ate dinner at her house almost every evening the second year of our marriage after Kathryn was born. Her basement housed our "free laundromat." She was with me in Texas for my brother's funeral, and we shared stories through the night after Busia died. We talked to each other every day. If there was nothing new to discuss we would say, "Just checking in." We got even closer after Cocia had a stroke, which left her paralyzed for three years. She passed away on July 6, 2005, but her love and spirit remains.

My Uncle Chester, lovingly called Che, was my first example of what a real father and husband was supposed to be. When his son dropped his ice cream cone, he didn't say, "That's what you get for being so clumsy!" as I'd heard all my life. Instead, he gave his little boy his ice cream cone. When his daughter, Debbie, was upset because she smashed up his brand new car, he told her, "You're much more important to me than that piece of metal." He supported Debbie when her husband died nine months after they married, and he cried with his youngest daughter, Sue, when her first son, Tommy, died from leukemia one week before his second birthday.

After my divorce, Uncle Chester stopped by my apartment on cold winter mornings to make sure my car started. He fixed my car for free when I was single and financially strapped. He was my aunt's caregiver for the three years that she was paralyzed. He never thought of himself, but gave up a big part of his life to take care of her; he never complained. He is a man of compassion and loves his children and family. Che, you're my hero!

Aunt Bernice and Uncle Chester's strong emphasis was, and still is, on "family." Their children Gregory, Debbie, Tom, and Sue call their dad and each other almost every day just to make sure that everything is okay. Greg and his wife, Maureen, bought a small home on the northwest side of Chicago. They gutted the whole house, leaving only the bathroom, one bedroom, and the living room walls standing downstairs. Then they added a large family room on the first floor and three bedrooms upstairs. This became a family project, and with help from some of their childhood friends, it took almost a year to complete. A couple years later, at Greg's daughter's graduation party, Greg took me aside and said, "The reason we left one bedroom downstairs was for you. If there comes a time that you can't take care of yourself when you get older, you have a place here with us." Although it's my intention to live independently in my own home until I die, like my friend Kay did, I was deeply moved by his concern. The loving hearts of my aunt and uncle have been passed on to all of their children.

My parents were the opposite of my aunt and uncle. Growing up, I admired my Aunt Bernice and Uncle Chester. They set a great example for me, and I know that the best parts of me evolved from spending so much time with them.

CHAPTER TWENTY-NINE

God gave me three Cates in my life, Katherine, Kathryn, and Catherine, but He only gave me one Richard, my second husband. God put all of life's finest qualities into this one magnificent man. His greatest God-like quality is that he has loved me unconditionally for the past thirty-one years. He has been my greatest supporter and encourager. He loves our daughter, Kathryn, and takes wonderful care of her.

Even though we tried to have another child after Kathryn was born, I was unable to conceive again. When Rich realized this, he decided to expand his influence with boys by becoming a director for the AWANA program at church. He has been in that position for twenty years. He takes personal interest in his boys. He attends some of their baseball games, soccer games, and basketball games to encourage them.

I must admit I had some prideful feelings when I overheard a conversation he had with one of the young men. Rich said, "William, you will be leaving the AWANA program this year and moving on to the teen youth group. You haven't finished your last book, and you need to do that to get your Timothy Award. You only have a couple weeks left to accomplish this. I've already ordered the Timothy Award for you. I'd like to come over and help you finish the last book so that you can receive it." William's mother overheard the conversation and was touched. She said she would make sure that William finished his book. Rich knew that William was conscientious about finishing up all the other books in the program. The Timothy Award was the highest honor in AWANA. He didn't want William to miss out. It was a proud moment for Rich when he watched William receive the award.

Rich has mentored other boys in our church. When one dad noticed that his son was struggling with self-esteem, he asked Rich if he would talk with his son. Rich took the young man out to dinner followed by other meetings, and their conversations were rich (no pun intended). Rich found out what was bothering him, and he was careful to keep their meetings confidential. He mentored and encouraged him through college. Every semester break, he visited and the two of them had dinner together. Four years later, he graduated from college and is continuing his education going for a doctoral degree.

Rich has discovered one of his spiritual gifts is encouragement, and he utilizes this God-given gift with young men and boys. He is respected as an AWANA leader. Though caring and encouraging, he is strict with the kids that attend the program. His capacity to show the AWANA children love and respect as they grow into Godly Christian men is clear.

Rich has a wonderful sense of humor. He keeps laughter alive in our family even through hard times and struggles. I always wondered where Richard and his sister, Marilynn, acquired their great sense of humor. It wasn't from their mother or father; rarely did either of them tell a joke. Rich's father was one of fourteen children. Rich said that when he was growing up, Sunday dinner was often at Grandma's, and the whole family came. Because of the large number of family members, there was a first and second seating for the meal. Funny stories and jokes filled the day while everyone ate, waited for the second seating to eat, or cleaned up after dinner. They always had a great time together. Shortly after we married, I met his aunts, uncles, and cousins at a family reunion. Almost fifty people attended the party hosted by his Uncle George and Aunt Pat. It was at this reunion I got to experience their humor firsthand. I could see how his family molded Rich's upbeat personality. Although most of Rich's aunts and uncles are deceased and these family gatherings aren't held as often, being together is still a memorable experience for all of us.

It's hard to be angry with someone when you're struggling to control your laughter. Dieting and watching our weight is continual at the Blasco household, but I always give up scolding him when he goes off one of our diets if he uses a few well-chosen, funny words. He knows it and uses it to his advantage.

Though Rich never seems to learn that I have a unique sense of knowing when he is cheating on a diet, he still tries to get away with those little deceitful times. Once he went to pick Kathryn up from the babysitter when I was working part time. The next day, I needed to use the van to go to the store. On the passenger's side of the car was an empty bag from Dunkin' Donuts. I asked him, "When did you buy donuts? There's an empty bag on the van seat." He looked at me like he was a small boy caught with his hand in the cookie jar and answered, "On the way home from Verne's, Kathryn pointed to Dunkin Donuts and said, 'I want a donut, daddy.' Now how could I refuse that?"

Rich is totally trustworthy and dependable if it doesn't involve food. He's my rock when I feel like I can't keep going. He pulls things together when I fall apart. If things rattle him, he never shows it. He takes things as they come and never complains.

Rich has always put me first in his life. From the first day of our honeymoon until this very day, Rich always makes me feel valued and loved. He says, "Just get what you like. If you like it, that's all that counts." He always wants to make me happy.

Rich worked hard for Kathryn and me throughout our married life. He retired January 2, 2007. A month before his retirement, he made me cry. He said, "Barb, when I retire I'm going to get up early every morning to take care of Kathryn and get her ready for the bus. You have been doing this for twenty-eight years, and now it's my turn."

Rich is a kind, loving, and caring person. Material things don't impress him. He is happy and content. I've never heard anyone say one bad thing about him. Everyone who meets him loves him. One of my greatest blessings has been having this Godly man as my husband.

CHAPTER THIRTY

As could probably be guessed, the fourth Kathryn who has impacted my life is our daughter. Although the doctors said she wouldn't live more than a week, she is now thirty years old.

Instead of being a "vegetable in the fetal position the rest of her life," as we were told at her birth by attending physicians, she is a loving, gentle young lady. She has a mild disposition and constantly smiles. She has never cried or had tears, even through her five surgeries. She sleeps through the night unless her scheduled pattern has been changed. If she happens to wake us up at night, a drink of water, change of diaper, and turning on soft music on her radio will keep her content and allows us to go back to sleep.

She seems content with her life, which makes it easier for us to cope. Kathryn, like the other three Kathryns, is strong. She, too, is a survivor.

It has been said that friends come in many varieties. There is the friend that comes into your life for a *season,* and then circumstances change and they are gone. Then there is a friend God sends into you life for a *reason,* to accomplish a certain goal He set for your life. When their job is done, they too move on. Lastly, there are the Proverbs 18:24 friends. They are the friends who stick closer than a brother. These are those life-long friends who are always there for you. They only leave you through death. All these friendships are important and special. I have encountered all three in my life, and I have cherished each and every one of them.

PART SEVEN

Godly Wisdom

Acquire wisdom! Acquire understanding.

Do not forget, nor turn away

from the words of my mouth.

Do not forsake her, and she (wisdom)

will guard you, love her,

and she will watch over you.

PROVERBS 4:5 & 6

My friend, Shirley, has a cousin with a disabled daughter in her fifties. The parents of this daughter have never taken a vacation, gone out to a movie, or taken time out for themselves. It does not have to be like that, and it doesn't fit with the abundant life God has for us with or without disabled children. Parents and families of the disabled don't have to be martyrs, and being a martyr could be the worst thing you can do for yourself, your spouse, your family, your friends, and for your special needs child. Everyone needs, and is entitled to, time out from the stressful days and responsibilities of everyday life. The story of Jesus going out into the desert for forty days and forty nights to get away is an example for us to follow. Our bodies are not meant to take a constant beating, physically or emotionally. A few hours or days away from your disabled ward will not hurt them, but it will be a big help to you, your spouse, and your family. When you are physically refreshed, it is mentally refreshing also.

Rich and I have a date night once a week. Our friend, Cate Fink, comes to sit with Kathryn so that we can go out and spend time together. She considers this a ministry and doesn't charge us for her services, a wonderful blessing for us. Besides our date nights, we take vacations. When money is an issue, we go somewhere close and inexpensive. With the divorce rate being as high as it is for marriages that have disability involvement, it is important to show your spouse how important and valuable you consider them. It's good for Kathryn also. She gets to experience another world meeting new friends and doing new activities.

Rich's father called me one day shortly after Kathryn was born. He was crying and said, "Please don't divorce my son."

I had no idea where this had come from. I asked, "What are you talking about, Dad? Why would I divorce Richard?"

In a broken voice he said, "Someone told me people with a disabled child get divorced because of the stress."

I reassured him. "Dad, don't worry about Rich and me. We have a strong marriage, and we need each other more now than ever. We're not going to get divorced."

I reassured my father-in-law, but I knew his concerns were realistic. Marriages in which a disabled person is involved, whether it is a child, dependent parent, or a spouse, have a high rate of divorce. One source cites the disability divorce rate at over ninety percent.

Disability is hard. Financial problems can be a burden on the whole family. Exhaustion can lead to discouragement and stress. When one cannot see a solution to the problem, they can become angry, bitter, and immersed in self-pity. Their attitudes change. Depression sets in. Friends start to stay away because they don't know what more they can say or do to help the situation. They feel helpless. It becomes a no-win situation as everything becomes overwhelming. Exhaustion is inevitable without some scheduled respite for the caregivers.

When churches take an active role in the lives of families with special needs people, they provide financial, emotional, and spiritual help. Our friend, Cate, is one of these church friends who has

made our lives easier and more bearable. Her volunteer care giving to our daughter has enabled us to get out at least once a week
and have time for each other. It is necessary, however, for families
of the disabled to let their needs be known to the church family.

People in our church have not only been encouraging and
supportive to Rich, Kathryn, and me, but also very generous to
us. There are two families whose generosity we will never forget.
John and Dee were the first to invite our small family of three
over to dinner, insisting that we bring Kathryn. Several times
after Dee died from cancer at age fifty, John called me and said,
"Kathryn has a birthday coming up. I want to take you shopping
for a gift." Several times, we went to J.C. Penney's, and I picked
out a top or a pair of pants for her. I held up something, and said,
"This is good." John said, "Keep going. You haven't reached the
budget I set for her gift yet." Each time we walked out of the store
with three or four outfits.

Knowing how much Kathryn loved being in his pool, John
often invited us to Sunday dinner and would say, "Bring your
swimsuits; we'll go for a dip in the pool after we eat."

John is a devout Christian and spends three days a week teaching Bible studies. One day after his wife died, a man approached
him and said, "I'm sorry to hear that you lost your wife." John
replied, "I didn't lose her, I know exactly where she is." Dee
accepted Christ as her Savior so John knew that she was in heaven
with the Lord.

The other couple, Jake and Juliann, did something similar.
For birthdays and Christmas, Juliann came over with several bags
of gifts. There were dresses, slack outfits and, one year, even a
beautiful down winter coat. Because Kathryn hasn't grown very
much, she still wears this winter coat today, years later. Besides
taking care of Kathryn's wardrobe needs, they often took Rich and

me out to dinner and the theater, entertainment that we couldn't afford back then when I wasn't working. Juliann has the gifts of giving and serving and she continues to use these gifts well. These days her ministry is to the needy people in Honduras. She makes two trips a year there, using her nursing skills to help the sick and administer medications when needed. She has inspired many in our church to make this mission of mercy with her.

Other families have sent generous monetary gifts to Kathryn throughout the years for different occasions. Rich and I can never repay these acts of kindness and generosity. We try to reciprocate by passing along these blessings to other less fortunate families in our disability ministry.

Involvement in a church with a disability ministry is a great help, and, from experience, I recommend it highly. If you are not connected with a church family or a friend who will help out, there are respite agencies to help pay for childcare. Take advantage of them if you can't afford to hire a sitter.

A date doesn't have to be fancy or expensive. In nice weather, pick up a couple of sandwiches and share a picnic in the park. Take a long walk or get ice cream. What you do isn't important; doing something together is. It's easy to get wrapped up in your disabled child and not take time for yourself and your spouse. Setting a top priority for your relationship can be your marriage insurance policy, benefiting you, your spouse, and your special needs child.

The Joni and Friends website (www.joniandfriends.org) can direct you to a church with a ministry to disabled people. The website and Joni's organization are both excellent resources for families with special needs. The phone number for Joni and Friends is (818) 707-5664.

With the help of family, friends, church, and other resources, as you and your loved ones begin to make time for each other, God works out the details. We became Christians, found Glenview Evangelical Free Church, and began attending regularly. Kathryn had one of her many surgeries and after her cast came off, she needed intensive therapy. The hospital gave us choices. We opted for the care-by-parent unit at the hospital, staying with Kathryn twenty-four/seven instead of going back and forth many times each day.

One evening during our two-week stay, after Rich arrived at the hospital to relieve me, an unfamiliar nurse walked into the room and greeted us warmly. "I'm Karen Alstadt. I go to Glenview Evangelical Free Church, and I'm a nurse here at Lutheran General. I read about your situation on the weekly prayer sheet. I'll stay and watch Kathryn so that you and Rich can go out and get something to eat. Stay as long as you like. I'm in no hurry to get home."

Before this angel of mercy's arrival, I had been having a pity party for myself. The weather was beautiful outside, and I resented being stuck in the hospital. Karen was more encouraging than she ever knew. God sent encouragement when we needed it most.

Dependency on God and recognizing the importance of the marriage relationship contributes to a strong marriage. Rich and I know this is just as important as the care we give to our disabled daughter.

CHAPTER THIRTY-TWO

Growing in grace and knowledge of the Lord is the goal of a Christian's life. Learning that God is always available is one of the lessons we've gleaned as we've aimed toward the goal of a deeper, more meaningful God-led life. He wants us to reach out for His help. Robert E. Mayer's article "Does Faith Make a Difference?" provided some wisdom for us.

Mayer says faith and love are two tired, dried out words saying little about reality. Living a life of inspiring faith is becoming rare in our society. After the tragedies in the mid 60's of the Vietnam War, the Kennedy and Martin Luther King, Jr. assassinations, we went through an era of disillusionment in the 70's. We lost confidence in almost everything: government, the church, big business, the great society, education, etc. We evolved into a society with profound skepticism. Nothing surprises us, and faith has given way to resignation.

Humans are goal oriented. Goals connect our experiences and give us meaning and significance. Faith defines our concerns and goals. Without faith, life becomes fragmented, disoriented, disjointed: giving way to emptiness, hollowness, and dissatisfaction. Life becomes full of experiences with no connection, a giant jigsaw puzzle dumped on a table with no rhyme or reason until it is assembled. Faith gives us a sense of fulfillment, wholeness, integration, and happiness. Mayer concludes saying, "Faith may not appear to move mountains, but it sure keeps the mountain from falling down."

CHAPTER THIRTY-THREE

As sometimes is the case, success comes with a high price. My grandparent's successful tavern business gave my dad access to all the alcohol he wanted. He started drinking as a teenager, which eventually led to his alcoholic addiction and health problems. My father's drinking at home caused havoc in our family. He was asthmatic and a heavy smoker; this further complicated his health issues. Dad's fragile lungs developed the more serious condition of emphysema. By the time I graduated from high school, Dad had suffered two heart attacks. The doctors indicated he only had a year to live unless he quit smoking and moved to a drier climate. My parents decided that Arizona was their best option, and they moved shortly after I turned eighteen.

Faced with life or death, Dad began to evaluate his life. My father could see he wasn't going to leave this world with much wealth if he died. He feared that his family wouldn't be able to manage financially without him. In his mind, he wanted and needed more money, and he needed it quickly. Gambling on horse races lost the two-flat building that my grandmother gave him where we lived. He lost all of the savings that he and Mom worked so hard for all their lives. He was penniless and had to borrow money to move to Arizona. His last ditch effort

for financial security for Mom and us failed drastically. My sister
and I were angry and decided to stay in Illinois, and we moved
in with our grandmother. We didn't want to have anything to
do with Dad for a couple of years. As I matured, I realized that
Dad's intentions were good, he didn't gamble to hurt us. He just
made a very bad choice.

Robin McGraw, wife of television's Dr. Phil, in her book,
Inside My Heart, talks about making life choices. Robin's childhood was similar to mine. Her father was an alcoholic and a
gambler, too. Her father drank and gambled away his paycheck,
staying away from home until he sobered up. My father wasn't so
considerate. He stayed home while he participated in his vices,
creating chaos and turmoil for all of us to witness.

Robin continues to write about another family member who
was irritating. She concluded, *"I could not control this person, but I
could control myself. What other people think of me or say about me
ought not to influence what I know to be true about myself. To doubt
myself because of what others think or say would be to hand over my
power to them, and that is something that I will not do. I never give
my power away."*

Problems in life don't disappear when a person draws closer
to God and walks step-by-step with Him. What can happen is a
change in attitude about the problems we face. We can choose
to let people, circumstances, or situations depress us or make us
angry, or we can choose to forgive and let go. We could be bitter
or better! Fortunately, I am learning to do the latter!

If we believe Romans: 8:28, *"All things work together for good
to those who know and love the Lord,"* we need to ask God to show
us what good can possibly come out of what we view as bad.

Looking back at all the "bad" things in my life, it's obvious
that good has come out of each experience. I've learned to look

to God for answers. As He revealed Himself and His plan for my life, I've seen a bigger picture. I am able to see the value of Robin McGraw's advice about not allowing other people to rob us of our power.

CHAPTER THIRTY-FOUR

Faith in Jesus Christ has made a big difference in my attitude and in my life. Without faith, I would be lost, depressed, and stuck in the dysfunctional world from which God saved me. In my totally self-centered world, I was convinced that my husband, daughter, and family would not and could not survive without me. I am convinced now that there is nothing in this world that isn't dependent on God. Miraculous changes take place when God takes up residence in our hearts.

When I'm down and depressed, I find the best cure for me is to reach out to people who have bigger problems than mine. I come home thankful for my life and situation. It's been said that feeling sorry for yourself is like a rocking chair. It gives you something to do, but it doesn't get you anywhere. Investing time and effort in others is the way to overcome, and it's much more satisfying.

Joni Eareckson Tada has said, "We're all disabled. It's just more obvious in some of us than in others." She also said, "Most people look at a wheelchair and see confinement. I look at my wheelchair and see freedom. If it wasn't for this wheelchair I wouldn't be able to get around and do the things I do."

I understand what Joni means. In 1996, when I went on a

Wheels for the World trip to Poland, we gave a child with brittle bone syndrome a wheelchair. The mother cried and said, "I thought that I would have to hold my daughter in my lap the rest of her life. We don't let other people hold her because in the past, they moved her the wrong way and they broke her bones. But, now she will be able to do things without me."

A few months ago, at a Joni and Friends fundraiser luncheon, a couple got up to speak and the woman said, "Our children aren't disabled, they are just differently abled."

It all boils down to one word; *attitude.* In his book, *Strengthening Your Grip,* Charles Swindoll wrote this about attitude. He could not have stated it better:

> The longer I live, the more I realize the impact of attitude on life. Attitude, to me, is more important than facts. It is more important than past, than failures, than successes, than what other people think or say, or do. It is more important than appearance, giftedness, or skill. It will make or break a company...a church...a home...a component.
>
>   The remarkable thing is we have a choice every day regarding the attitude we will embrace for that day. We cannot change our past...we cannot change the fact that people will act in a certain way. We cannot change the inevitable. The only thing we can do is play the one string we have, and this is our attitude.
>
>   I am convinced that life is ten percent what happens to me, and ninety percent how I react to it.

We live in a different era than our parents and grandparents. If we named the era we live in, I would choose to call it the "disposable era." We have disposable plates, cups, dinnerware, bowls, diapers, etc. We have a mentality that thinks everything is disposable. Often we lack the patience and contentment it takes to develop a long, lasting relationship. When patience and contentment diminish, it often results in a disposable marriage.

Contentment seems to be a lost art in this disposable era. We have a tendency to look at people who have more than we have. When we do this, we feel cheated, deprived, and sometimes jealous. We need to be looking at people who have less, seeking ways to contribute to the comfort and well being of those who are less privileged.

First Timothy 6:6–11 says, *"But godliness actually is a means of great gain, when accompanied by contentment. For we have brought nothing into the world, so we cannot take anything out of it either. And if we have food and covering, with these we shall be content. But those who want to get rich fall into temptation and a snare and many foolish and harmful desires which plunge men into ruin and destruction. For the love of money is a root of all sorts of evil, and some by longing for it have wandered away from the faith, and pierced themselves with many a pang. But flee from these things, you man of God; and pursue righteousness, godliness, faith, love, perseverance and gentleness."*

Can it be that we are more focused on material things than on Godly endeavors? Without adding God into the equation, there is no true happiness or contentment.

CHAPTER THIRTY-FIVE

In 1994, Reverend Scott and Janet Willis lost six children in a tragic highway accident on their way to Wisconsin to celebrate the birthdays of two of their children. The Willises had nine children; three were adults and the six younger children ranged from thirteen years to six weeks old. They lovingly referred to this age gap as the "A" and "B" teams.

My first encounter with Janet Willis was when she spoke at a dinner banquet after the accident. Janet home schooled their young children, which gave her more quality time with them. She and Scott had severe burns after the van caught fire, but those scars eventually healed. The incredibly difficult healing was in coping with the loss of all six of their youngest children. Janet quoted Job 1:21 from the Old Testament, *"The LORD gave and the LORD has taken away. Blessed be the name of the LORD."* The Bible says that we are to praise God in all things. As hard as it was, she realized that this included praising God even at the accident scene. She knew in her heart that God was in control and that He was good. She also knew the children had accepted Jesus and were safe in their heavenly home with Him.

I was impressed with Mrs. Willis that evening and prayed about asking if she would speak at our H.I.M. support group meeting the next month. I did call, and she accepted my invitation and gave a beautiful testimony of her dependency on God.

After the meeting, we talked and Janet invited my pastor's wife, Ann, and me to her home for lunch. We arrived at the church where she and her family lived in rooms that previously had been used as Sunday school classes. While Ann and I were with Janet, she shared stories about her children and how hard it was to go on with life without them. Imagining her loss helped me see how essential it was that Scott and Janet not waiver in their trust in God. They looked to God, and He sustained them during this time of grieving. At that time, she had no idea how God would use this great tragedy.

In the next year, events began to unfold that were unexpected and shocking. The Willis' vehicle had hit a piece of debris dropped from a truck driven by Ricardo Guzman. He had received his commercial Illinois driver's license after bribing an official in the Illinois Department of the Secretary of State. Because he could not understand English, he was unable to heed the warnings from other truck drivers who noticed the metal piece dangling from his truck. The scandal uncovered many illegal practices and involved people all the way up to the office of Governor of Illinois, George Ryan. There was a lengthy trial and Governor Ryan was convicted and is serving time in prison.

The Willises saw how the accident that caused the deaths of their innocent children eventually helped make our roads safer.

Scott and Janet Willis will always grieve the loss of their six children. Nothing can change that, but their faith holds their lives together. They turned the evil into good when they started a foundation to help others in need with the money awarded to them by the court for their personal injuries and the wrongful deaths of their children.

The Bible tells us we will go through trials. Trials are compared to fire. When it is said, "I've been through the fire," it can mean Satan has put trials on our path in life to deter us from doing God's work. Could it be if we are going through "the fire," it is because we are actively involved in advancing the Kingdom of God? In our situation with Kathryn, as I've gone through trials I have grown closer to God and have learned to trust Him more.

A television preacher once said, God allows those fires for different reasons. Sometimes only He knows why. Watching the news of the great infernos burning in California, the fire fighters often set backfires that burn toward the main, greater blaze. Those backfires serve an important function. When the two meet, the main fire has no fuel to continue burning and will eventually die out. As Christians when we are "on fire" for the Lord, we provide our own backfire for those trials we experience in life. The Bible, the Word of God, gives us fuel for our internal flame. As our fire within becomes stronger than that which comes from the world, we can survive anything Satan throws at us, and his evil plan will backfire.

Trust and obey. This might be the hardest commandment in the Bible. It's easy to trust and obey God when life is good. If we face no illness, our husband has a good job, all our bills are paid on time, and we are enjoying good health, trusting God is easy. The added bonus of enough money left over for a vacation and the fun extras we've come to expect is icing on our cake.

Though much of life is uplifting and positive, because we are human, we know we will experience the unavoidable, inevitable, hard times. So, when our world dishes out the "not so good," what is our reaction? Hopefully, we don't get mad and blame God, or stop trusting and obeying Him because He's "let us down." We might give in to the lie that God doesn't care and move away from

Him, but God remembers those who serve and obey Him faithfully. Those who love, fear, honor, and respect Him even though they feel they got the short end of life's stick are blessed and loved by God. A reward is promised His children, but it is not guaranteed on Earth. That is reserved for eternity in Heaven.

Contrary to what some believe, Life, with a capital L, is precious. God does not weigh His children on a scale giving some a higher rating than others depending upon their usefulness or mental abilities. When each of His children come into the world, they are precious to the Heavenly Father, no matter what their cognitive reasoning skills might be. God cares about those in the lower ranges of the scale as much as He does His precious high achievers. In heavenly terms, there is no such thing as a one to ten evaluation.

So, living with a mindset that one is a victim, less loved by God and Man, is senseless. Those who choose to live with a 'victim' mentality are doing just that...wastefully choosing their own lot in life. Regardless of one's circumstances, as Children of our Heavenly Father, we ought not allow our lives to be defined as wounded or suffering.

For the many years I wrestled with God and asked Him why He hated me, valuable time and energy was wasted. I knew I wasn't perfect, but I was also certain there were other people a lot worse. Struggling back and forth with a wounded self worth was useless. Wondering why God was giving me all these bad things in my life caused me to waffle in my faith, in my effectiveness, and in my self-esteem. I knew everyone had a few trials in life, but by the age of forty-two I felt I'd had more than my share. Finally, I received Christ into my heart in May of 1986. It was after that He showed me that there was a purpose for all these bad things in my life. He showed me that His grace was sufficient, and nothing else was necessary. I must trust and obey Him, and He would make everything clear. Thankfully, through God's grace, I learned my lessons and am still on that road of growing and learning. His grace is giving me strength to keep going, determination to succeed and continue learning the lessons He knows I need to learn. With each new lesson, I'm gaining stronger faith and allowing God firmer control on my life. I see He is able to turn something bad into something good, and my surrender shows me answers to my "Why me?" questions. I know this kind of grace comes from Jesus alone. Trust and obey. The two hardest words in the Bible. But, if practiced, you can be sure that you will have the rich life God intended for you.

Reading the Bible gives Rich and me strength and wisdom. In Psalm 37 it says; *"How blessed is he who considers the helpless; The Lord will deliver him in a day of trouble. The Lord will protect him and keep him alive, and he shall be called blessed upon the earth."* This promise in the Bible has been fulfilled in our lives. God has seen us through many trials and continues to do so. How awesome to think we are blessed because of our caring for Kathryn.

The Bible has been my guidebook. It is the way God speaks to me and indicates how He wants me to live my life. When I am fully surrendered to His will, I allow my Bible to lead me day by day. I rejoice that God thought enough of Rich and me to entrust our Kathryn into our care. All the hard times are erased by the joy she has brought into our home.

In all things, give thanks. Most of us will never experience the great loss the Willises had. I pray that when trials do enter our lives that we will have the courage of Scott and Janet and praise God in every situation, no matter how devastating it may be, trusting that God sees and knows all things, and He will get us through all the bad times.

CHAPTER THIRTY-SIX

My favorite classic movie is "It's a Wonderful Life." Jimmy Stewart played the part of George, a kind and generous man who did wonderful things for all the people in his home-town of Bedford Falls. His trial came when a deposit that his uncle took to the bank got lost. The bank examiner was coming that day to the savings and loan George managed. This missing deposit could put George into jail. He wished he had never been born. God sent an angel to grant him his wish. George visited a world in which he didn't exist. The angel showed him how ter-rible the lives of his friends and family would have been had he not lived. At the end of the movie, all of the people he helped pitched in to pay the loss. He wasn't a wealthy man, but he was rich in friends.

This movie reminded me of the influence Kathryn has had on the lives of other people, disabled or not. I would like to think that though she can't talk or walk, she has helped people both directly and indirectly. Mentoring, support groups, wheelchairs, medical equipment, and so many other services have made a dif-ference in the difficult circumstances of many families. Kathryn's influence even prevented a mother from aborting her perfectly healthy and normal daughter. Seeing our family and how we've handled our situation has shown others that with a positive attitude, seemingly impossible trials are manageable. What I first thought was a punishment from God, has turned out to be my greatest joy and blessing.

Each of us has different talents, different dreams, and different destinations, yet we all have the power to make a difference in someone's life. Kathryn's life is no exception. **She has made a difference.**